Loving Inward, Living Outward, Looking Forward

LIFE LESSONS THAT ENLIGHTEN, ENCOURAGE, AND EMPOWER YOU TO REGAIN CONTROL OF YOUR LIFE

BRITTNEY PRESSLEY

Loving Inward, Living Outward, Looking Forward
published by:
Brittney Pressley
Alexandria, VA

Edited by Tanya Davis-Northern
Cover Design by Mark Davis
Author Portrait photographed by Timothy Davis

ISBN: 978-0-9890345-0-0 (sc)

ISBN: 978-0-9890345-1-7 (ebk)

TO VIEW MORE WRITINGS BY THE AUTHOR:

http://mind-does-matter.blogspot.com

Printed in the USA by
Morris Publishing®
3212 E. Hwy 30 • Kearney, NE 68847
800-650-7888 • www.morrispublishing.com

This book is dedicated to my mom,
Tanya

Acknowledgments

My tremendous faith in God
Is what has carried me this far
And continuing to be faithful
Is what really makes me a star

I have so many people to thank
Some are related, some are not
Some are younger, some are older
But all have contributed to my thoughts

All have contributed to who I am
All have contributed to my foundation
All have contributed to my growth
All have contributed to my salvation

From aunts to uncles to mentors
From grandparents to teachers to cousins
From siblings to colleagues to friends
From me to the dozens and dozens

Of people that have believed
I sincerely want to thank you
For if it wasn't for you all
I would have never had a clue

I would have never had direction
I would have never stood up tall
I would have never gained the confidence
I would have never, never at all

Became who I am today

I would have never gotten through
I would have never, I would have never
Gotten to where I am without you

Contents

Section III: Looking Forward

Introduction

Throughout the course of our lives, more times than we can count we will be confronted with the opportunity to answer the question "who are you"? When interviewing for a new position, when tapping a stranger's shoulder mistakenly thinking it is a friend, or when we are on a spiritual journey to reveal purpose. It is impossible to live a rewarding life without knowing who we are and what purpose we serve. It is also impossible to truly love anyone unconditionally if we have not learned to love ourselves first. The processes of *loving inward*, *living outward*, and *looking forward* will help to overcome life's many challenges, to live and love freely, and to fulfill our life's purpose. There are lessons that accompany each process; lessons that I have learned first-hand, through numerous books that I have read, and vicariously through family, close friendships, and the more than occasional random conversation with a complete stranger.

The process of **loving inward** begins with...love. Before we can be madly and deeply in love with another human being, we need to first be madly and deeply in love with ourselves. Loving ourselves encompasses the understanding that although each of us is imperfect, we are still worthy and deserving of happiness. In order to ensure happiness, we must realize that happiness is not a goal. Growing up, my mom would always say, "Every choice has a consequence", and happiness is most certainly a choice – a choice, that is accompanied by positive consequences. But before we choose to be happy, it is essential that we rid ourselves of negative thoughts – "I'm not good enough", "I can't", "I'm too afraid", "What if it doesn't work out?", "I'm never going to find love", "I can't ever forgive them for what they did to me". When we have these thoughts, we are hindering ourselves and creating a blockage to forward progress. We are in control – we are good enough if we think we are, we can do what we think we can, we can choose to be brave rather than fearful, it will work out if we believe it can, we will find love if we open ourselves up to it, and we can forgive if we realize it's not for the other person but rather for our well-being.

The process of **living outward** begins with…love. After we have learned to love ourselves unconditionally, we should then be able to love outwardly – to forgive, accept, and inspire others. In other words, living outward is a reflection of our relationships. How we treat people and view the world around us is a direct reflection of how we view and treat ourselves. Is it reasonable to accept only our flaws and not another person's? Is it reasonable to treat people the way they treat us? Is it reasonable to forgive ourselves for making mistakes but not forgiving others for the mistakes that they make? Genuinely appreciating and loving others for who they are, and not for what they have, are two of the greatest gifts that we can give. Encouraging and supporting others on their journey, without expecting anything in return (or being so engulfed in our own lives) are other gifts that we can give – free of charge and with a dual benefit. Life is not just about our personal growth; but rather how our growth impacts the world.

The process of **looking forward** begins with, you guessed it, love. Learning to love and appreciate life's rocky roads and vowing to learn from every success and failure will create ultimate bliss. Understanding that every situation that we have been placed in, every person that we have met, every obstacle that we have faced, every job that we have held, every detour, up until this very moment, has been no coincidence. Our past helps to shape us, but we are only defined by the past if we allow ourselves to be. The ability to dream big, have a plan, and appreciate the storms is what looking forward is all about. We should never feel stuck because, again, we are very much in control. If our path takes us down a dead end street, we have two options – 1) *do nothing*, sit there and complain that we chose an incorrect route, and start a barrage of insults to ourselves because we made a wrong turn, or 2) *do something*, turn back around, keep driving until we reach our destination, and promise ourselves that next time we will pay better attention to the signs that led us to that dead end. Our destiny is in our hands, well rather, in our hearts. Let's open our hearts, get in control and make our lives, and in essence, the world better – together.

Section I: Loving Inward

Lesson 1

El-Oh-Vee-E (Love)

Take care of yourself
Before you take care of another
You should help yourself
Before being a keeper of your brother

Meaning a brother's keeper
I could get a lot deeper
Or do you get the point?
Let this be the grim reaper

The death of your insecurities
The death of your impurities
And the birth of your surety
The birth of your security

Being secure in who you are
Both inside and out
But inner certainty is so necessary
Without a shadow of a doubt

The ability to love ourselves is where it all begins. Each of us is beautiful, unique, and gifted in our own way so we should tap into ourselves and realize what it is that we have to offer the world. Each of our lives serves a purpose! We are worthy of receiving love no matter our circumstances; however, before we can accept love we have to first be open to receiving unconditional love from ourselves. We set the example of how others should treat us, how others view us, and how deeply others can love us.

We should never surrender to our wrongdoings because the truth is that no one is perfect. We have each made mistakes and we will continue to do so; yet, we are still worthy of receiving love. Low self-esteem, negative thoughts, and a negative self-image all interrupt our ability to fully love ourselves. True internal love is arriving at the point in which we can look in the mirror, acknowledge that we are not faultless, accept that we are not faultless, and still flaunt a confident smile.

All too often, self-worth (internal love) has been substituted with the words 'conceit and egotistical'. By no means is the act of wanting to love and accept who we are the same as being conceited or egotistical. In fact, conceit is defined as an "excessively favorable opinion of one's ability, importance, wit, etc.[1]" Self-worth has

---

[1] Dictionary.com; http://dictionary.reference.com/browse/conceit?s=t

nothing at all to do with excessiveness or opinion, but rather everything to do with necessity and truth. Being secure in who we are does not equate to cockiness or an egotistical attitude but it reflects the necessary level of comfort that we need in order to embark on our journey towards long-lasting internal, eternal love.

Lesson 2

Happiness Comes From Within

The possessions, the money
The houses and the cars
Won't make you really happy
If you don't know who you are

No one can complete you
If you don't complete yourself first
Until you figure that out
The pain will keep being dispersed

Happiness hasn't been hiding
You just never knew where to look
You've been praying and searching
And reading all sort of books

You haven't looked to yourself
To make your own self fulfilled
Hold yourself accountable
And then work to rebuild

Note to self: Happiness cannot be purchased, happiness is a choice, happiness lives within each of us, and happiness is free.

One of the biggest mistakes that we can make is to place value on a possession or responsibility on a person to determine and control our happiness. When searching for temporary fulfillment, having an intimate fling, buying a new pair of shoes or a new piece of jewelry may do the trick. But when searching for happiness and longevity, the responsibility needs to be placed onto us. All too often, we end up disappointed, hurt, and bitter because we relinquished our happiness into the hands of another person. How could we possibly be disappointed, hurt, and bitter when we made a decision (consciously or subconsciously) to allow someone to dictate how happy we are or aren't?

Internal happiness derives from being comfortable in our skin, freeing our heart of hate, not worrying about what anyone thinks of us, and having a passion. It also derives from the understanding that we have a choice to either be happy or miserable. Happiness most certainly sounds and feels better than being miserable! Life is so incredibly precious and wonderful; happiness should be a given. Unfortunately though, it may be difficult to see 'life's preciousness' when 'life's ugly' takes center stage. Fortunately for us, determining to see ourselves through the ugly and still muster a smile is still our choice!

If we step outside of our circumstances from time-to-time and speak in depth with others about their journey, we would understand that each of us has gone through trials and tribulations. Our stories, journeys, and obstacles may be completely unrelated but we can become connected through our choice of overcoming obstacles and sustaining happiness. Any place worth going will have its ups and downs – and sometimes its dead end roads but we are the drivers.

We must also be aware that happiness is not a state at which we can ultimately arrive but rather a daily option. When we wake up in the morning, we *choose* to brush our teeth (I hope), we *choose* to shower, we *choose* which outfit to wear, we *choose* to eat breakfast and we can also *choose* to be happy. Happy that we are alive, happy that every day that we wake up we have a chance to create a new beginning, happy that we are still standing after being dealt blow after blow, happy that we have the free will to make a choice to be happy.

Lesson 3

Invest In Yourself

Take a look into your portfolio
Is it as diverse as it should be?
The portfolio, meaning your life
Don't get confused with the terminology

Are you giving back to others?
Are you living with an open heart?
Are you getting to know yourself?
And not letting someone tear that apart?

Are you trying to make a difference?
Are you having tons of fun?
Do you laugh until it hurts?
Do you put yourself as number one?

Your life is the biggest investment
That you could ever invest in
This is no wheel of fortune
Your own wheel you have to spin

Investing in a 401(k) or a 403(b) is the norm in the working world. We put money away for when we retire so that our retirement can potentially be less stressful, at least financially. It is suggested that our investment portfolio be diverse in order to properly allocate risks, which in return yields higher earnings. If we decide to modify our portfolios at any time or are in need of one-on-one consultation, there is typically an option to schedule an appointment with a Retirement Counselor via our employer.

If we think of our lives as our portfolios, is it as diverse as it should be? Do we invest in our well-being - health, mind, and soul - as consistently (or inconsistently) as we contribute to our savings plan? Do we take the time out to consult with a professional in the event that we decide our lives need modification? In the midst of the world's chaos, it can be easy to lose ourselves in daily routines of work, parenting, marriage, financial woos, and the list can continue on forever. There comes a point, though, when we need to take a step back from the chaos and find ways to revitalize ourselves. This does not make us horrible employees, parents, spouses, or negligent citizens but what it does is make us responsible and liable for taking care of ourselves.

Since we know that we need to love ourselves before we can be loved, and find happiness from within for it to be long lasting; we also need to invest in ourselves before investing financially or investing our time in our many commitments. Financially speaking, our investments can suffer if we have a lack of financial knowledge; the same goes for investing in ourselves. If we are unaware of that 1) it is absolutely necessary to invest in our well-being and 2) how to invest in our well-being, our well-being would essentially be subpar. When investing the majority of our time in something or someone, without thinking to invest our time in ourselves, it can be detrimental to our health as well. Think of it this way: we can have a substantial amount of money being invested for retirement, and we can invest our time in many activities but what good is a substantial amount of money and a packed schedule if we are stretched thin and emotionally drained? Investing in ourselves includes taking time out to rejuvenate (daily, weekly, or monthly), recover, and restore. We need to clear our minds, cleanse our souls, and find ways to live healthy, or healthier, lives.

Lesson 4

Be Yourself, Not Who Others Want You To Be

There is only one you
One, your point of view
One who walks in your shoes
The one can change and get through

Being our authentic selves takes substantially less effort than pretending to be someone that we aren't or being the person others would like for us to be. Our uniqueness and individuality makes us special, why should we then conform to someone's view of how we should act, speak, think, dress, handle our finances, and raise our children? Our individuality may make others uncomfortable – maybe we are too boisterous, or too shy, or too confident, or too self-efficient for their liking – but the price that we will pay for not being true to ourselves is enormously high. Let's say, for example, that we decide to change the way we act for another person; it won't be long before they aren't satisfied and request that we change something else and then something else again. When someone wants us to change, or conform, it has everything to do with them wanting control and not feeling comfortable in their own skin; and nothing at all to do with us.

How interesting would the world be: If we all looked the same? If we believed in the same religions? If we had the same upbringings? If we had the same political views? If we listened to the same types of music? If we drove the same cars? If every town or city looked the same? If we enjoyed eating the same types of foods? If we watched the same television shows? If we acted the same? Not very interesting at all! The reason that we appreciate different cars, different foods, different television shows, different cities, different political parties, and different types of music is because of the distinctiveness of each, and the free will to choose which one(s) we like out of all of the options that we are offered. We should also appreciate the same about ourselves. The distinctiveness that each of us offers, the free will that we have when it comes to choosing a career, a place to live, friends, religious views, political affiliates, and so on. There may be people that we naturally connect with, share similar mentalities with, and share similar interests with but there is no one else in the world that can replicate our authentic selves; no one! Embracing our individuality is an essential step in the process of truly loving who we are.

Lesson 5

Confidence Is Key

But this is not Bible preachin'
Rather internal reachin'
And confidence teachin'
So your confidence peaks n'

You experience the greatest love
The kind you are worthy of
You may think you are undeserving of
Because of all of your wrongs but they aren't indicative of

Who you really are
As the purest you
Minus the hats you wear
I'm talking when you are bare

I'm talking inner love
I'm talking inner beauty
I'm talking inner love
I'm taking inner beauty

There is nothing wrong with confidently presenting ourselves to the world. If we are not confident in our abilities, how can someone else be confident in our abilities? If we do not believe in ourselves, how can someone else believe in us? If we do not trust ourselves, how can someone else trust us? The answers to all three questions are the same – they can't! All too often, a confident person may be deemed 'cocky' because of the way that they walk, speak, dress, and assert themselves in a situation; there is a distinct difference however.

Confident individuals are certain of their abilities, poised, humbled, levelheaded, and assertive. Cocky individuals are pompous, overconfident about their abilities, not poised, assuming, bigheaded, and aggressive. Cocky individuals are so absorbed in their own lives and accomplishments that they do not have time to recognize that other people exist in the world. Because confident individuals are levelheaded, they can appreciate others alike and even assist those who are less confident in becoming more certain and poised.

A confident aura simply states, I am not perfect but I'm still great. I will give my all no matter how high the stakes and I won't back down because I dictate my fate. Without confidence, there is not much that we can successfully accomplish. Confidence is essential when we are interviewing for a job, attempting to land a promotion, selling a product, driving, giving a presentation, disciplining a child, learning a new skill, negotiating, so on and so forth. Without confidence we will seem unsure of ourselves, flaky, unenthusiastic, passionless, and as if we are lacking direction.

Holding our head high does not equate to thinking that we are better than, but that we are confident in our ability to never give up until we become better and better. Behind the scenes, our self-confidence works overtime to convince and reassure us that we are worth it; that we have every right to celebrate who we are. Each time that we have succeeded or approached a great feat there were many hurdles that stood in our way before the celebration could occur.

When we are putting our time and energy into working towards an accomplishment, it is imperative that we are confident of the path we take and of our abilities and resources to assist us on our journey. It doesn't seem sensible to work hard and take steps in a direction if we are not completely confident. We will have overcome a tremendous amount of insecurities and turbulence before proudly flaunting our self-confidence – no one can take it away from us!

Lesson 6

Accept Your Flaws

Stop being so critical, cynical
And analytical of yourself
Accept yourself flaws and all
Now that is true wealth

Not talking dollar signs
That undermines
What wealth actually means

I'm talking value
And confidence
And everything in between

We have a dire tendency to bash and criticize ourselves due to the fact that we aren't perfect – but haven't we already acknowledged that no one in this world is? Before we took our first breath the intricate details of who we are today were already predetermined. This includes, but is not limited to, our height, facial features, behavioral traits, personality, hair color/texture, and predisposition to medical conditions. But for some reason, we become fixated on why we don't have a smaller/bigger nose, curlier/straighter hair, lighter/darker eyes, fewer/added inches in height, a different personality, etc. How can we even contemplate the idea that the beauty of our existence was an error? By no means does this imply that we can't wear contacts to change our eye color, or put perms and relaxers in our hair, or wear makeup, or wear a shoe that gives us a few extra inches; but it does imply that we need to accept who we are, how we look, without any additions or subtractions. The inability to accept our imperfections is damaging to our self-esteem. It can also allow for jealous or resentful emotions and behaviors to surface, with us wishing that we looked like someone else, acted like someone else, walked, talked, and had the same personality as someone else.

Accepting who we are and how we look does not imply that transformation is not warranted. Change is what makes the world go round! If there are certain things that we do not like about ourselves, we have the power to change them. If we want to drop a few pounds, we can eat healthier and/or begin an exercise regime. If we don't like our poor financial management skills, we can enlist the help of a professional and/or educate ourselves on better ways to save or invest money. If we would like to become more outgoing or social, we can join different social groups and/or enlist the help of our socialite friends for tips. If we don't like our inability to prepare a tasty meal, we can search for recipes to follow and/or take cooking classes. There are hundreds, maybe even thousands, more of these "if, then" statements but once we recognize and accept our imperfections, we will free up more room for growth and become much more comfortable in our skin. We look the way that we do for a reason, we were given specific talents for a reason, and we are who we are for a reason!

Lesson 7

Forgive, Forgive, Forgive

An action that seems so easy turns out to be so rough,
So we step out on faith and leave karma up to us,
For us to teach that person to never hurt us again,
Whether it be a mother, a boy/girlfriend, or a friend,
We carry around the burden until it weighs us down,
To the point where our once glowing smile has turned into a frown,
The echo of the pain gets louder by the hour,
Until our tender love has disappeared and has left us feeling sour

Learning to forgive may be one of the most essential lessons that we need to learn in order to completely free our minds, hearts, and souls. Holding onto the hatred and resentment does not rectify the situation, does not change what happened, nor does it hurt the person who caused the pain. Forgiveness has everything to do with us, *everything*! While we walk around bitter, miserable, sad, hurt, and angry, the other person is continuing to live their lives. Forgiveness does not justify a behavior or situation but it allows us to move on with the lesson(s) learned from the heartache.

Forgiveness can be broken down into a two-part process: forgiving the other person and forgiving ourselves. The benefit of forgiving the other person is to take our control back. When we are angry at or hurt by someone, the longer that we hold onto those emotions, the longer that person has control over us. If we were to see or speak with the person who hurt us during a time that we are still in pain, the sight of them and sound of their voice would most likely bring about pure irritation in us. The benefit of forgiving ourselves is to exonerate thoughts/feelings of guilt and shame. We cannot continue to bask in blame and hold ourselves accountable for an event that happened in the past. We cannot control the actions of others and we cannot control what has already happened; but we can make a decision to regain our control – now!

If we accept that every situation that we have been apart of and that every person that we have encountered up until this point in our lives was intentional, we should then be able to forgive a little easier. No matter how painful or horrible the situation was that we found ourselves in, we deserve to be unchained from the pain. Hidden in every situation is a lesson that can be learned and if we can uncover the lesson, it can help to carry us forward and assist in allowing our hearts to be reopened. Forgiving allows us to be liberated, yet wise. After all, when the word 'forgive' is broken down into its two syllables, for give, it translates to: *meant to grant.* Which interprets forgiveness as intentional.

With forgiveness comes great responsibility; this is why we should carefully think through our healing process. Once we make the decision to forgive, there should be no second-guessing; forgiveness is a final decision! We should not renege on our forgiveness and if we ever find ourselves doing so or thinking twice about doing so, it's because we weren't ready. It also indicates that our original act of forgiveness wasn't sincere. As forgiveness is for our well-being, it would be beyond counterproductive if we forgave with leverage. Meaning that we forgive with ulterior motive, in hopes that the person we are forgiving is at our mercy. Forgiveness is pure and should have no strings attached. Once we forgive we will feel light...freed...pain free.

Lesson 8

Fear Is Poisonous

After your uphill battle
You may have some bumps and bruises
But you know a scar will scab
And a bruise will always heal
And a bump will go away
Are you nervous still?

No person, animal, or situation can make us fearful without our consent. Fear is simply an impediment to our routines and overall growth. Even with that, constant feelings of anxiety, trepidation, and worry enter in and out of our lives and cause interruptions. These emotions deter us from being our authentic selves because they control our thoughts and actions. We have all experienced disruptive fear at some point in our lives; fear of an animal, fear of death, fear of being hurt, fear of someone, fear of making mistakes, fear of not being accepted, fear of being let down, fear of not being good enough, fear of change, fear of being alone, fear of the truth, fear of disease, fear of being misunderstood, or maybe even fear of being who we truly are. Although some fear is necessary as it allows us to protect ourselves from threatening situations, the quandaries ensue when our lives are consumed with fear.

An overabundance of fear is certainly limiting and unhealthy! We cannot become the person that we so desperately want to become if we welcome toxicity into our lives. Fear is a manipulator – it takes us out of character and convinces us that we are supposed to be continuously fearful. It makes us second-guess ourselves, it causes our hearts to beat rapidly, and it hypnotizes us to believe that we do not have the determination and strength to overcome it. We have plenty of willpower to regain our control and overturn our fears.

We all experience different levels of fear, still, fear is in fact poisonous if it is continuous and allowed to interrupt our routines. Once we recognize what or who is causing us to have these emotions, we can then go about handling them on our own, with a support group, and/or with professional help. It is imperative that we stand up to our fears and take our control back; we owe it to ourselves. On its own fear can be powerful, but we are much more powerful without it.

Lesson 9

Grow and Become The Best You

You don't have to be who you've always been
Just because you've always been
The new you is already there
You just need to look within

And shed the outer layers
Commit yourself to making a change
Just know you can only change but so much
Who you really are stays the same

But don't lose sight of the final goal
Since growth is certainly inevitable
You cannot grow and live in the past
That's like trying to eat something inedible
Once you grow it feels incredible

It is easy to remain comfortable and complacent in life but change is inescapable. We are all in charge of becoming the best person that we can possibly be since growth is a fundamental part of life. We can read books until our eyes burn, take classes until we have learned, save up all of the money we have earned, but following our heart should be the main concern. All too frequently, we focus on becoming the best parents, the best friends, the best lovers, the best employees, and being in the best shape without being our *best selves* first. Being the best at anything comes from within – "How bad do you want it?" is the question that we need to constantly ask ourselves.

The person that we all want to become already lives within us. In order to grow and become the best person we can possibly be, we need to get rid of the internal contamination that pollutes our spirits (fear, not accepting ourselves, negative thoughts, pain, etc.). The next step would be to work towards becoming the friend we would want to meet, the parent we would want to nurture, love, and teach us, the lover we would want to support and comfort us, the employee that we would want to hire for our business, and get in the shape that we would want our personal trainer to be in; this will serve as an invaluable gauge.

Thinking of personal growth in totality can be daunting, so it may be ideal and more manageable if we create smaller goals that ultimately add up to our bigger picture goals. It would also be helpful if we tracked our growth week-by-week, month-by-month, or year-by-year so that we can observe and celebrate how far we have come. Although life is not a sprint but rather a marathon, we still need to get organized, set our goals, and condition ourselves so that we can successfully cross the finish line. The greatest component of our growth is that we do not need to search high and low for transformation; we can just start from within until we are fulfilled. We will always have room for more learning and for more growth, so we should never become complacent on our path to becoming the best us.

Lesson 10

Uphold The Golden Rule

If two wrongs don't make it right
Then that should be all you need
To never intentionally cause harm
Your pride should not supersede

What you know is true already
Don't stoop down to being petty
Just be real with yourself
Don't fake it like Machiavelli

When a person does you wrong
You know karma is coming to them
But as soon as you retaliate
Just know it's coming around again

Then the vicious cycle begins
Round and round it goes
Until everyone is worn out
Now who delivers the last blow?

The 'golden rule' is a concept that we were all taught, hopefully, in elementary school; "Do unto others as you would have others do unto you". We should treat others the way that we would like to be treated and not the way that they treat us. This may sound like it doesn't make sense – if someone does us wrong, why should we do right by him or her? Doing right by someone has less to do with him or her and more to do with us. We already know that we cannot control the actions of others but we have full jurisdiction over our actions. With this, and absent of solely wanting good karma in return, we should always treat people the way in which we would like to be treated. The reality is that not everyone will be appreciative of our kindness and not everyone will treat us with the upmost respect but this does not give us a valid reason to be rude and malicious.

There comes a point when our willpower of upholding the golden rule is more important than the response that we will receive from doing so. Think of it this way; when we are entering into an establishment and decide to hold the door open for the person behind us there will always be a few people who don't say thank you – should we allow those few people to deter us away from holding the door open for anyone ever again? Without knowing the response we will get, we should still hold the door open because it is polite. This is what the golden rule is all about – *our intentions and actions.*

People who intentionally take advantage of others, who are spiteful, purposely hurt others, and manipulate because they can, may seemingly be difficult to deal with as they tend to get under our skin more often than not. We should still treat these individuals with respect no matter how nasty they are to us. Respect is something that we all want so we should therefore always be respectful. There is a difference, however, between the golden rule and allowing ourselves to be taken advantage of and continuously used. We should quickly distance ourselves from those negative types of people, as they are tremendously toxic to our well-being and progression.

There is no doubt that upholding the golden rule sounds easier than it may be to carry out through action but in the end it is so worth it. As we are accountable for our actions and how we present ourselves to the world, it is essential that we always act in a way that we would want mirrored back by others. While this may sound cliché it is true that what we put out comes back; how we treat people is how we will ultimately be treated. Since our actions dictate how we will be treated, it becomes that much more vital to uphold the golden rule.

Lesson 11

Move On/Let "it" Go

No one said life was easy
There are no rainbows without rain
It's more satisfying when it's rough
There's no happiness without pain

You can't get to the top of the mountain
If you don't sweat and climb and climb
As long as you're climbing upward
What's the sense of looking behind?

Moving forward isn't easy
But you are certainly worth it
In fact deep down you already know
You just don't know what your worth is

As we enter into unfamiliar territories along our journey towards growth and internal liberation, moving on and letting go of the past can be terrifying. No matter how painful our pasts may have been, it can be comforting to stick with what we already know. Even our current situations can be comforting although we may be in an unhealthy relationship, in a job that makes us miserable, or in a financial situation that is less than manageable but moving on and letting go makes us both stronger and wiser. Simply put, holding onto the past, grudges, guilt, anger, pain, and regret are all holding us back. It also hurts those who truly care about us but it certainly hurts us the most. Living in the past places limits on our futures.

It is normal for feelings of angst to creep up as we venture forward. Any type of change tends to bring about a plethora of emotions, both optimistic and pessimistic, but we decide which emotions will dominate. We have no control over what has already happened but we can vow to learn from and appreciate the past as we move forward. We should become agents for change not practitioners of the past because tomorrow hasn't come and yesterday already passed, and although tomorrow isn't promised we can make ourselves a promise that as we look forward we won't take a look behind us.

Moving on and letting go doesn't mean that we are in denial or that we are attempting to erase our past memories, but what it does is deny and erase any situation or person that no longer serves a beneficial purpose in our lives to affect us or have control any longer. Tomorrow is a brand new day and overcoming obstacles equals growth, we can either move on or stay behind but know that we cannot do both. Moving on can seem unnatural depending on our mentality; it sure is a lot harder if we aren't concerned with practicality. We deserve to move forward and not be consumed or surrounded by negativity. We deserve to see what our futures have in store. We owe it to ourselves to let go of any emotion or circumstance that has a chokehold on us because we can do better; we need to do better.

Lesson 12

Be Faithful, Not Wishful

Faith versus wishing
Conviction verses hope
That's a solid versus a liquid
Wishing is like a shower without soap

Meaning we would never get clean
Faith is the substance that we need
To cleanse and purify ourselves
Being wishful doesn't guarantee

That anything will ever work out
Because we're wishing upon a star
Waiting for the clock to strike 11:11
Is not what will get us very far

Faith is like having an extra backbone
It holds us up and keeps us strong
Wishing gives us hope for days
Faith lasts all life long

In the context of loving inward, the act of being faithful is not in the realm of showing loyalty to a romantic partner; though it is a respectful and upright action to follow. Faithfulness in this sense has to do with believing and engulfing ourselves in a force much greater than us. Being faithful is not about religion in and of itself and is in no way judging which religion is more superior or effective but rather the holistic idea of believing in a higher power; whatever it may be. Faith gives us stability, resilience, a reason to live, something to look forward to, something to believe in, strength, direction, and truth. Wishing gives us hope but not substance.

There is nothing wrong with making a wish or being hopeful but faith is what will make us feel whole. The difficult aspect of faith, however, is that we cannot see, feel, or measure it and therefore relying on it makes it easier said than done. What makes wishing easier is that we can do so when the clock strikes 11:11, when we blow seeds off of a dandelion, when we blow our loose eyelashes, when we wish upon a shooting star, when we see a red bird, when we have a four-leaf clover in our possession, when we blow out the candles on our birthday cake(s), drop coins in a fountain or wishing well, hold our breath under a tunnel, and send a message in a bottle. Yet, faith is much stronger!

Faith has no gimmicks, no superstitions, monetary or materialistic value attached to it but it does show up every day if we embrace it and allow it to fully permeate through our lives. Aside from faith's many benefits, it can teach us that situations happen the way that they're supposed to and that there is a larger purpose for why we are living – much larger than we can ever fathom. It also teaches us to follow our hearts and allow ourselves to be guided by a superior force, even if we cannot see it. When we become completely and authentically connected with a higher power we will certainly feel how reliable and powerful faith really is.

All in all, wishing is not stable. Faith has nothing to do with fables, meaning it is all about truth and letting us know that we are able. To achieve whatever we put our mind to and to weather each and every storm, with the courage to remain ourselves never needing to follow or conform. With faith we cannot worry because it doesn't work that way. Should we pray and expect the worse or not worry at all and still pray? Wishing is clearly more mystical but is wishing more logistical? Without having any faith we can be declared egotistical because we can't move forward alone. We need faith right by our side; the fun is that we can't see it and it will still serve as a guide.

Lesson 13

~~Self-Pity~~

The mud I am referring to
Is the kind we all go through
So don't go looking for pity
Just because somebody hurt you

It's all a part of life
Learn to overcome the pain
Turning tragedy into triumph
Is the name of the game

You can learn from every obstacle
From every rough and windy road
From every time you wanted to give up
Scream, yell, or unload

Be thankful for the lessons
Even if some lasted longer
Because what doesn't kill you
Will definitely make you stronger

Feeling bad for ourselves or allowing others to feel bad for us is destructive in every way. Pity and shame are of no positive or helpful value as we venture towards inward love; self-pity allows us to harp on the past and opens the door for excuses. The reality is that each of us has gone through tribulations and we will continue to go through them for as long as we are alive. True strength comes from overcoming any obstacle that is thrown or placed in our way. Being shameful or blameful won't make us true fighters; it actually weakens our mental stability and allows for stagnation.

The word pitiful, which derives from the word pity, is associated with synonyms such as cowardice, misery, suffering, low, deplorable, woeful, pathetic, paltry, and wretched. Do you want any of these words to describe and/or define you? Do any of these words sounds like they will make you happy, fulfilled, or enthusiastic? Do any of these words describe people that you would like to spend time with? Do any of these words sound like they would change the outcome of any situation? Do any of these words make you feel empowered? Do any of these words sound like they will help you love yourself deeply?

Once we realize that we have full control over our emotions, pity should take a back seat – or rather be thrown out of the window! In order to fully love and embrace ourselves, we need to get rid of any sentiment that works against our progress; pity being one of them. There is no need to feel bad for our circumstances or ourselves since we are drivers of change. And we should most certainly not allow others to feel bad for our circumstances because although it may be comforting to have someone acknowledge our struggle, it is not beneficial if we remain stuck there. Turning misfortune into fortune takes time but it is absolutely doable if we set our mind to it. Knowing that no storm, so to speak, lasts forever should give us enough reason to happily climb over hurdles and leave pity behind.

Lesson 14

Don't Ask "What If"

What if we did not make excuses for what didn't happen?
What if we used what didn't happen for motivation to make 'something' happen?
What if our hearts were pure?
What if our actions matched our intentions?
What if our lives were filled with love?
What if we laughed more?
What if we weren't so hard on ourselves?
What if we weren't so hard on others?
What if we saw every tribulation as a part of our growth?
What if we promised ourselves not to live in the past?
What if we promised to give our all?
What if we lifted others up instead of putting them down?
What if we learned something new every day?
What if each one taught one?
What if we leveraged our strengths and creative abilities?
What if we were honest with ourselves?
What if we were honest with others?
What if we experienced more joy than stress?
What if we lived in the moment?
WHAT IF...

What if the world wasn't round? What if you were born to different parents? What if you were born five years earlier? What if you were born as the opposite sex? What if your name was different? What if you graduated from a different college? What if you went to college? What if you were born in a different town, state, or country? What if you had different friends? What if you were a few inches taller? What if your eyes were a different color? What if your hair was a little longer, shorter, thinner, thicker? What if you weren't so lonely? What if you were more outgoing? What if you weren't the black sheep of your family? What if that horrible 'thing' from your past never happened? What if you weren't exposed to abuse at a young age? What if you never got a divorce? What if you got married? What if you stop letting your fears get in the way of your potential success? What if you were hired for every job that you interviewed for? What if you saved more money while you were still living at home with your parents? What if your parents didn't kick you out of the house? What if you had another child? What if you could have children? What if we all looked the same? What if we all had the same beliefs? What if we all agreed on every topic? What if we were all perfect? What if death wasn't a part of life? What if life wasn't a part of death? What if we experienced no pain? What if the roles of women and men were reversed? What if there was no such thing as terminal illness? What if money did grow on trees? What if the apple did fall far from the tree? What if life was fair? WHAT IF?

It is so tempting to become fixated on what could have happened or what did not happen that we could easily lose sight of what actually happened. We are all guilty of asking "what if" at one time or another because it allows us to wallow in fantasy. There isn't anything wrong with fantasy but we should be aware that the longer we fantasize, the less time we spend confronting reality. When we ask "what if" it is typically for situations that are out of our control. 'What if', like self-pity, does not solve anything; it does keep our mind spinning in continuous circles though.

Looking back to reflect on what we could have done better is fundamental for forward progress but to solely focus on what went wrong and on "what if" is not helpful. Completely accepting the way we are and the situations that happen to us should alleviate the need to ask 'what if', but it can be complex. We have an instinctive need to question our decision-making and to fix things that we believe are broken. We ought to understand that things happened the way that they were supposed to, we can only learn from our past decisions/actions, and asking "what if" will not fix anything that is broken. If we journey through life allowing ourselves to embrace what happens around and to us there should never be a need to ask "what if". If we position ourselves to grow and experience illustrious opportunities there should never be a need to ask “what if”.

Section II: Living Outward

Lesson 1

El-Oh-Vee-E

Once we fully love ourselves
We can fully love another
Everything we do for ourselves
We can then do for others

First accepting then forgiving
Then inspiring and admiring
From the purity of our hearts
With our love never expiring

Then trusting and lusting
And understanding but not demanding
From the bottom of our hearts
While our love keeps on expanding

The ability to live outwardly points toward our relationships with others and how we present ourselves to the world. If and only if we have made the choice to effusively love and accept ourselves we can then do the same encompassing other folks. It is much easier to accept someone after we have accepted ourselves; to teach someone how to be confident once we have found confidence; to forgive someone after we have forgiven ourselves; to invest in someone after we have invested in ourselves; and to find people who contribute to and enhance our happiness after we have found internal happiness. This elucidates why loving inward is consequently vital.

How we view the world, our family and friends, our jobs, our children, or our pets is how we view ourselves. Loving ourselves opens our hearts to love and see the true beauty in the world around us, our family and friends, our jobs (or allows us to determine that our current job is not fitting enough), our children, and our pets. Closing ourselves off to love doesn't allow us to fully embrace the beauty that surrounds us. When we love ourselves deeply, we can see the beauty in anything and anyone – even the person who has caused us the most pain. Loving ourselves also allows us to understand that each person in the world has a story, a journey, idiosyncrasies, and has gone through tribulations just as we have; and we can then begin the process of outwardly accepting, embracing, and loving.

The same goes for pity, respect, trust, and admiration. When we reject self-pity – respect, trust and admire ourselves we can then do the same for others. If we do not respect ourselves can we logically respect someone else? If we do not trust ourselves can we logically trust someone else? If we do not admire ourselves can we logically admire someone else? If we pity ourselves can we logically encourage someone to not pity him or herself? Love is our nucleus – it is the most pure and sincere emotion that we can feel, sense, and share. We must truly love before we can truly live!

Lesson 2

It's The Small Things

It will always be the little things
That brings a smile to our face
And when we do little things for others
We better the human race

There is nothing wrong with extravagance
Or indulging in lavish things
But remember less is more
As long as our thoughtfulness has no strings

Attached to it I mean
Smiles shouldn't be few and far between
Because it's the smallest thing we can give
Especially when they are unforeseen

Just when you were going to give up on the entire human race; when you had enough of the negativity, someone held the door open for you before you walked into a store, or said please or thank you on a day where you thought everyone else forgot their manners, or told you that they loved you, or that they appreciated you, or let you merge into traffic after everyone else ignored and rode past, or brought you a knick knack in your favorite color, or said "Good Morning" with a genuine smile while everyone else walked by concentrating on getting to their destination! How did any of these gestures, or any others that you can think of, make you feel? Would you like to experience that feeling more often than not? Going out on a limb and assuming that it was a refreshingly amazing feeling, this proves that the smallest gesture or gift can warm our hearts and bring the largest smile to our faces! It is only fitting that we pay kind gestures back (or rather forward) and extend our kindness to other people.

We never know when someone is having a bad day or is feeling down and could benefit from a smile, nice card, or a simple hello. The small things that we do for other people (or that are done for us) speak directly to the popular expression 'less is more'. This concept can be difficult for us to completely grasp due to the extreme emphasis that society, our friends, peers, family, and maybe even that we place on materialism – what we have, how much we have, and/or how much it costs. In all actuality, an invaluable gesture from a complete stranger can outweigh a lavish materialistic present from someone in which we are familiar. This is not to say that lavish gifts are unimportant and should not be appreciated or that gifts from strangers are more important than those given by our friends but no price tag can be placed on a considerate deed.

When we are seeking out a way to outwardly and merely express ourselves to someone that we care about, for example, we should not overextend our minds with trying to find or come up with the most extravagant, perfect, or expensive gift. As long as our giving comes from the heart - the thought, rather than the gift, becomes the focal point. Think back to the nicest thing anyone has gotten for you. Do you focus on how much it costs or how it made you feel? Think back to the nicest gesture that someone has shown you. Do you focus more on the gesture itself or how it made you feel? Think back to a time when someone appreciated something small that you have done for him or her. How did that make you feel?

Lesson 3

Embrace Change

We know that change is inevitable
But it can be hard to embrace
Change happens all of the time
And things feel like they are displaced

Because we tend to ward it off
Based on how it makes us feel
But if we learn to embrace change
We would stop spinning our wheels

Change is what helps us to move forward
Change is what helps us to keep growing
Change lessens boredom
Change also lessens plateauing

"We must become the change we want to see"
Thanks Mahatma Gandhi for that advice
Accepting change is necessary
Staying stagnant for life will not suffice

If change does not take place, by default, everything and everyone would then stay the same; how much fun would that be? Change exists all around us and keeps our lives interesting, teaches us lessons, and allows for continuous opportunities to occur for our growth. Yet and still, learning to accept and embrace change can be a challenge. Change can make us feel uneasy, anxiety-ridden, unsure of ourselves, and frightened as it leads us into unfamiliar territories; but it is such an enormous part of life that we are left with no choice but to embrace it. Of course our other option is to reject change and remain the same in a world that is incessantly evolving.

Since change is constant, we would need to remain flexible in our journeys. We could then use the same flexibility when dealing with people that we know and don't know and/or in situations that unexpectedly arise. The concept of embracing change encompasses the most miniscule to the most extravagant types of changes. From noticing that we forgot our wallets at home after we are steps away from our destination, to getting a new haircut, to locking our keys in the car, to totaling a car, to starting to cook a meal and realizing that we ran out of a key ingredient, to last minute alterations to weekend plans, to taking on more responsibilities at work, to the death of a loved one, to growing apart from family/friends, to getting married or divorced, to accepting a new job, to moving to a new town/state or country, to our children growing up; the list can continue on indefinitely.

If we view any type of change as inescapable, and as a necessary component of our growth it may be easier to accept and embrace. We may not know when change is headed our way, what it will consist of, or how it will impact our lives but when we embrace the fact that no matter when change happens we will deal with it head on, then we will always essentially be ahead of whatever the actual change is. The moment that we decided to stop living in the past, we simultaneously agreed to accept whatever change would be thrown our way, whether the agreement was conscious or subconscious! Progress embodies change, this should not seem strange and if we do not want to become deranged then we will have to rearrange – our thoughts toward the present, and our thoughts while looking ahead because change embodies life and we should not ignore it and be misled.

Lesson 4

Practice Selflessness

Let's lend a helping hand
And expect nothing in return
Life is about giving back
Without hesitation or concern

The overall act of selflessness
Makes us more holistic
It makes us altruistic
It doesn't need to be ritualistic

But it should be simplistic
Being selfish gets us nowhere
Giving back makes us feel good
And lets others know that we care

Selflessness does not require a broadcast
Giving back does not take an audience
It is the right thing for us to do
And it should be as common as sense

The act of selflessness embodies understanding that the world is much larger than us. True selflessness can take the form of a gesture, gift, or deed. Once we truthfully understand this notion, we can then take action and express our selflessness outwardly. Actually, before we get going we should first know that selflessness should stem from a quiet heart; meaning that as our actions come directly from our hearts we are not to expect recognition or accolades in return. Acting or giving from our hearts and then expecting recognition simply cancels out the thoughtfulness of the act; the reward for being selfless is adding virtue and joy to our lives and to the lives of those we are touching. Being selfless does not indicate that we should ignore our needs and put everyone before us, but it signifies that there is at least one opportunity each day for us to genuinely help someone else without thinking about ourselves. No matter what our situations consist of, there is always someone who is in a worse predicament – therein lies our opportunity to be led by our hearts and greatly impact the life of another. Even if there is an opportunity to impact someone's life who is not less fortunate than we are, we should still embrace it.

If our actions are guided by our hearts and not by our eyes, and we don't give with any motives but we give in disguise; then we can either plan it out or let it be a surprise and encourage others to do the same - creating allies; and if we act on any opportunity that may arise we can turn somebody's lows into their highs. Selflessness is also about us learning to be more well-rounded and noble. To do something for someone, that they are unable or do not think about doing for themselves, brings about one of the utmost feelings. It also allows us to step outside of our circumstances and established routines and open up to another person's circumstances. We will never be able to walk a mile in someone's shoes, so to speak, but this should not deter us from viewing life through another's heart. When we are in tune with ourselves it is much easier to be in tune to our surroundings and the people around us. We may not know what someone's heart desires but it is not necessary to know in order to be thoughtful.

We should be aware of the fact that we only have control over our thoughts and our actions – not how either is received by the recipient(s). No matter how genuine we are when attempting to help another person, our intentions may be misinterpreted and our action(s) rejected. This could most certainly sting and hurt our feelings but it should not discourage us from acting selflessly again! The world desperately needs more selfless acts and more selfless individuals to infiltrate every neighborhood, school, and business in every city/town, state, and country. Similar to any other action or skill, selflessness can be learned if practiced continuously; we just need the desire to learn.

Lesson 5

Don't Drain Your Circle

We all have an inner circle
These are the people who keep us sane
The ones there to support us
And who listen to us complain

But if we are not careful
We could one day ruin ties
If we bombard our inner circle
This should come as no surprise

If we are ever in a true bind
We should seek help from a professional
Yes, our friends pose as moral support
But they are not to replace a confessional

We need to have some respect for them
And not drain our circle away
These are people we chose wisely
So we obviously want them to stay

The amount of people in each of our circles will vary but nevertheless we all have an inner circle that we confide in. These are people that we not only trust but enjoy being around, share similar interests with, speak for hours with, laugh until it hurts with, and also share our darkest moments with. We have a natural inclination to rely so heavily on our inner circle that we may not realize where the boundaries lie. Our circle does not exist for us to dump our every emotion, thought, or dilemma on; one of the many purposes of our inner circle is to serve as a foundation.

If we begin to dump an exorbitant amount of our concerns or problems on the people that we rely on and care about the most, our circle will slowly dwindle away or consequently become strained as some people will become fed up with our constant discarding. No one enjoys being dumped on! Not even the person that seemingly listens to our troubled stories or every rant. Some people are more tolerable than others but we have to know when to draw the line. For each person in our circle, the boundary will be different but either way we need to respect that we each have our own issues to deal with. This is not to say that our closest confidants can't assist us with working through our most difficult issues, but there comes a point where we should seek professional help if our problems become too consuming; support groups, therapists, Psychiatrists, counselors, and specialized doctors can aid us during difficult times.

We should remain cognizant of the 'information flow' from us to our inner circle, as to prevent potential dumping and draining. We each may be guilty of overloading our circle at one point or another but it is not too late to reevaluate our closest relationships; having open dialogue regarding boundaries might be the best starting point. Even if we occasionally catch ourselves indulging in an elongated outburst or story, we should always make our inner circle aware that we appreciate them and that our intentions are not to drain or dump.

Lesson 6

Their Problem Is Their Problem

Mi casa es su casa
But their problem is their problem
And we shouldn't make them ours
Using our energy trying to solve them

We can act as a sounding board
And even offer sound advice
But we need to stay in our lane
Or we will ultimately pay the price

We should not drain our circle
And our circle should not drain us
But when we care and love so deeply
Not draining can truly be tough

Each of us should remember
That we all have our own mess
So we should focus on our own troubles
This would then minimize our stress

Now that we know how important it is to not drain our inner circle, it is as equally important that we do not allow our inner circle to drain us. Their problem is their problem! It is not our responsibility to go around solving, taking on, or becoming stressed out about anyone else's problem(s) and vice versa. Quite honestly, it is tough not to take on the problems of those who are closest to us when we care and love them so deeply. Our natural instincts may even lead us to bite off more than we can chew when acting as a support system but we should take heed.

The more time we spend solving another person's problems, the less time we have to solve our own. This does not make us selfish or insensitive but we each have to own and be accountable for our issues! At times, taking on someone else's problems as our own can allow for us to take a much-needed break from our realities – *escapism.* Trying to escape or avoid having to deal with our realities only adds to our disarray.

The same guidelines that apply for us to not drain our inner circle applies to our inner circle not draining us - support groups, therapists, Psychiatrists, counselors, and specialized doctors can serve as an aid during difficult times. We should not be shy about encouraging the people in our circle to seek professional help should we feel like they are in need. Our encouragement should be accepted as long as our intentions are pure and our advice is genuine but we cannot focus so much on how it will be received. After all, these are the people who know us the best so they should be well aware of our intentions. It can be extremely painful to not take on the problems of the people whom we love, especially if they have serious troubles that need tending to and we feel that we have the resources, money, or knowledge that can help them; but we cannot care more than the person who the problem is directly impacting.

Because we appreciate our circle so much and they appreciate us the same, we should all remain conscious of whether we are appropriately nurturing our relationships and not being insensitive or disregarding one another's feelings. The moral of the story is that we should cherish our inner circle enough to not drain or dump on them and strongly encourage our circle to work within the same principles for us.

Lesson 7

Two Ears, One Mouth

The best things come in two's
We identify them as pairs
So it should be no shock why
We have one mouth and two ears

Listening is for paying attention
Hearing is for receiving noise
If we wisely choose to listen
We can then speak with poise

Ears are made for listening
Mouths are made for speaking
But if we use our ears just to hear
We will then begin critiquing

SHHHHHH!!! More often than not we should practice opening our ears instead of our mouths. Having two ears is truly a gift and we may not be utilizing them to their fullest potential. Our ears serve two functions: hearing and listening. The difference between the two is that hearing allows us to receive sound and listening allows us to take in and analyze what we are hearing. Simply put, when we are talking, we are not listening; when someone else is talking and our sole focus is on formulating our response, we are using our ears to hear but not listen.

We would be surprised by what we could learn if we utilized our listening skills more. If we think about how a successful therapist operates, we can identify that first and foremost his or her listening skills are astonishing. The way that they nod their heads and listen to our every word; take the things that we say and ask specific questions to gain further information; and most importantly the way that they never judge a word that comes out of our mouths. What therapists do not share with us about their success is that listening takes skill – great skill! Therapist or not, in order to be totally tuned into what someone is saying, without formulating our thoughts, judging or interrupting them, it takes practice. On the contrary, it is frustrating when we are trying to clear our minds through venting and the person we are speaking with is hearing rather than listening. They can also leave us feeling belittled with their seeming disregard while we are talking and merely expressing ourselves.

We have to determine when speaking or listening is more appropriate for the situation that we are in. We will never learn any lessons while our mouths are moving; we will learn plenty while our mouths are closed and we are listening. Listening requires both discipline and patience so that we can ultimately understand what it is that we are hearing. Receiving sound does not require any focus whatsoever. Frankly, the majority of the times that we are being called upon to act as a sounding board, the person who is speaking would prefer it if we listened more and offered advice less as he or she most likely has their mind already made up on what actions they will take. The better listeners we become, the less talking that we will do, which means the more we will learn so that we can sharpen our point of view.

Lesson 8

Be Genuine

Being genuine encompasses authenticity
Being genuine encompasses respect
Being genuine encompasses listening to our heart
Being genuine makes us appear suspect

If people don't know our intentions
If they think we have ulterior motives
It is up to us to share our intent
So that other people know it

Genuine acts come from the heart
We act on what we know is right
We know it's right by how it feels
Because it feels like we are guided by a light

That points us in the right direction
And never allows us to go astray
If we practice being honest and sincere
We will feel joy as if in a cabaret

When we are genuine in every aspect of our lives, we will feel a level of liberation, tenderness, and satisfaction that is unmatched. If we allow our authenticity to guide our thoughts, words, decision-making, and actions we will not be misled. Once we determine that we will live our lives in a genuine manner, there is no room for second-guessing our thoughts, words, decision-making, or actions. Being genuine does not imply that everything will always go our way or that we will always be right; it reiterates our pure intentions and realness.

Genuinely presenting ourselves to the world will attract other genuine folks, which will allow for our warmth to be felt. We will also attract those who are not genuine and who are oblivious of our intentions; we need to distinguish and separate both types of people. Those who are not genuine should not dampen or dissuade us from being our true selves but we should certainly keep our distance, as they will surely hinder our growth. These people may even leave us feeling as if we are not sincere because they may question or challenge our intent; we should not tolerate anyone who second-guesses our intentions. Those who are genuine will encourage us to grow and inspire us to do even better, without having said one word. We can draw from their honesty, feed off of their positive energy, embrace their sincerity, and together create synergy.

Our genuineness can take form as a kind

deed, advice, gifts, altruism, love, or affection to name a few. If our acts of sincerity are led directly by our hearts, we will forever be pointed in the right direction; we will know it is the right direction by how it feels. In order to know how *it* feels, our hearts have to first be pure and we have to be in tune with our thoughts and intentions.

Lesson 9

The Truth Will Set You Free...Literally, It Will

The funny thing about truth
Is that most of us cannot handle it
We'd rather hear a white lie
Or have the truth mixed with wit

So we don't have to feel the sting
But the truth is that truth hurts
It's not supposed to look pretty
But even a flower is planted from dirt

Before we can go preaching truth
We need to be honest with ourselves
Take a long look in the mirror
And take our feelings off the shelves

When truth is mixed with a kind heart
It loses some of its bite
Makes it easier to swallow
Empowers us with useful insight

The truth is that if we lie to ourselves it will be effortless to lie to others; if we are honest with ourselves then we can easily be honest with others. Seems simple, right? The truth can be complicated though. "Don't fix your lips to tell a lie", we were told this in our youth. "If you don't want Pinocchio's nose you should always tell the truth"; "Honesty is the best policy and the truth shall set you free but please don't be too blunt because there will always be debris." So if we understood correctly we should have been honest but not too much, we should have always told the truth as long as we were adding a soft touch! What this really means is that the truth is not the truth if we have to chew it up and then serve it on a spoon. It is not hard to understand that we shouldn't hurt each other's feelings but if the truth is covered up, are we truly real in our dealings?

Many of us grew up having been taught an ambiguous meaning of *truth* – we should have practiced telling the truth as long as it was within the guidelines that were set for us. For example, if we spilled our dark colored juice on the light colored living room carpet after we were told ample times to only drink our juice in the kitchen, we would then be expected to fess up, take accountability for our actions, and tell the truth. On the other hand, if one of our teachers asked why our homework had not been completed for class and we answered, "I didn't feel like doing it because I thought it was pointless", our honesty would surely be turned against us in the form of scolding or punishment; probably both depending on who our caretakers were. There are an endless amount of 'truth' contradictions that we may have experienced throughout the course of our lives but the truth, the honest truth, will set us free.

Truth personifies life. Life personifies reality. Reality personifies authenticity. Authenticity personifies genuineness. Genuineness personifies legitimacy. Legitimacy personifies validity. Validity personifies truth. Truth personifies life. Life personifies living. Living personifies existing. Existing personifies breathing. Breathing personifies air. Air personifies energy. Energy personifies liveliness. Liveliness personifies spirit. We personify spirit. We personify life. We personify truth.

Now that we know that the truth is inescapable, it is time for us to wholly embrace it. Similar to happiness, the truth isn't hiding; it has always been there – right in front of our faces and also inside of us! Compared to lies, the truth is much easier for us to recall and recant because it does not change; lies, on the other hand, can evolve into a bigger lie that evolves into a much bigger lie that can then evolve into a web of lies that cannot be unwoven. The truth will leave us feeling complete and lies will leave us feeling broken; truth will make our hearts feel at ease and lies will make us more outspoken.

Because we have to get our point(s) across before someone tries to call us out, but if we always told the truth we could speak with assurance and not with doubt.

Lesson 10

Enjoy The Beauty of Where You Are

Hakuna Matata
Carpe diem friends
Life is so much fun
Until the day it ends

No one gets out alive
Not the criminals or the Priests
Not the rich or the poor
Not the beauties or the beasts

Not me or you
Not she or he
Life is just so precious
Just look around and you'll see

Those who have been fortunate enough to possess the financial freedom to travel and see different parts of the country or world have seen true beauty – beautiful people, the beauty of dissimilar cultures, architectures, towns/cities, and foods. Fortunately, we do not have to travel hundreds or thousands of miles to admire true beauty as it surrounds us every day. When we can see the true beauty within ourselves the world suddenly becomes beautiful; people whom we have known for years appear more beautiful; strangers seem like they are more approachable; our neighborhoods appear more beautiful; our conversations become more appealing; our outer beauty takes on a brighter glow; our pasts seem dimmer; our futures seem to glimmer; our positive attributes come to the forefront while concentration on our flaws takes a backseat; nature's beauty becomes breathtaking; and our energy and aura become ultimately enhanced. Seeing the beauty in ourselves is our choice. Seeing the beauty in others is our choice. Seeing the beauty in life is also our choice.

The meaning of 'beauty' will not be the same for each of us; this contributes to our uniqueness. Nevertheless, beauty still exists around us if we choose to open our eyes, minds, and hearts wide enough. Beauty is deeper than what we see on the surface – beauty has depth and complexity. People, paintings, cultures, writings, songs, food, landscapes, and photographs for example all have depth and complexity; we decide how deep we want to perceive, explore, and analyze. Holistically, beauty allows for exploration, configuration, inspiration, ideation, innovation for each generation, integration, education, meditation, communication, observation, recreation, fixation, translation, celebration, syndication, concentration, dedication, consolation, correlation and maybe even deformation or imitation.

Once we are able to enjoy the beauty around us, we may think twice about booking that exotic vacation – well, on second thought maybe not! The point is that we can feel rejuvenated and gain appreciation for the beauty that not only exists in other parts of the world but for the world in which we have created for ourselves. Beauty can be illustrated through all five senses – sight, hearing, touch, smell and taste – and we should utilize as many as we possibly can. Our eyes, ears, hands, nose, and mouth determine beauty – we determine beauty.

Lesson 11

Know Your Strengths

Everyone was born with weaknesses
We tend to speak of them a lot
Everyone was also born with strengths
We tend to act like we forgot

But our focus should be reversed
Our strengths will open many doors
If we focus solely on our weak areas
We will face-plant onto the floor

Not all of our strengths equate to passion
Yet and still we need to be attentive
Because our strengths will help to shape us
This should give us extra incentive

To always put our best foot forward
And acknowledge that we are strong
Every person in this world has strengths
Knowing this we can't go wrong

Every person in this world was born with strengths, knowing this we can't go wrong! We are all great at *something* we just have to uncover what that something is. Actually, we each have a multitude of strengths that are ready to be awakened. Focusing on perfecting our strengths is far more productive than focusing on and depicting our weaknesses. Without identifying the specific details of our strengths, simply knowing that we have the potential to be astonishingly talented if we apply ourselves should enthrall confidence and enthusiasm upon us. Understanding that each of us has strengths should also assist us in looking past another person's flaws or weaknesses. Even the person that irritates or infuriates us every time that he or she opens their mouth has the potential to be astonishingly talented.

Being knowledgeable about the strengths that were gifted to us not only contributes to our confidence and provides us with the opportunity to make a living doing what we enjoy, but our strengths also benefit others. No matter what our forte consists of, there is someone's life who can be impacted by our skills – be it baking, or singing, or managing, or designing, or caregiving, or cleaning, or telling jokes, or mining. Our strengths play a much larger role than we could ever imagine hence the reason why it is vital that we put ourselves in situations that align to our strengths. Truthfully speaking, if we are continuously in situations that expose our weaknesses there is no potential gain for us or anyone else. Comparable to beauty, our strengths also have depth and complexity as they can be applied in different aspects of our lives. How we assess and break down our strengths is up to us so as long as we are first consciously aware that we have them.

Once we identify what our strengths are we can greatly impact the world! Our strengths are the skills that come natural to us; they place us in our comfort zone, lift us like we are on a thrown, give us definition like muscle tone, and enough strength to not be overthrown. When we recognize that our strengths are gifts then there should be no 'maybes', 'buts', or 'ifs' that the world should catch our drift, as long as we are clearer than a hieroglyph.

Lesson 12

Be Grateful

No one owes us anything
So we should always be grateful
When things don't go our way
We shouldn't resort to being hateful

Be thankful, be thankful
For the blessings, for the lessons
Be thankful, be thankful
Never letting our appreciation lessen

Doesn't matter if we are receiving a gift
Or simply a kind gesture
We should show gratification
Whether the giver is an investor or jester

We should be gracious and vivacious while our hearts are open and spacious, and know that we are truly one of a kind and that no one can replace us. We should always show our gratitude with respect and latitude for any gift or kind gesture via our attitude. If we are thankful, truly thankful, we will feel at ease and tranquil because being bitter will most certainly overflow our tanks full. With anger and disgust and annoyance and distrust but sincerity is a must and depending on the day it can be tough. Because life keeps throwing lemons so we duck and try to hide, which makes us feel like we are bound instead of bona fide. But we owe it to ourselves and we owe it to the world to show our true appreciation no matter how far that we are hurled. Being thrown around in circles doesn't give us a valid excuse to be ungrateful and hateful thus we need to call a truce. Since every situation has a lesson, as does our every interaction, both can add up like addition if we can take away from them like subtraction. But why punish a close friend, our family or a stranger solely because we are in a bad mood and cannot control our anger? As long as we are breathing we shouldn't whine like we are teething, we should save ourselves the trouble as our complaining needs sheathing. That just means it needs a cover for us to uncover our graciousness, which will add to our faithfulness, our aura and our bliss. No one owes us jack, it's a fact it's true, we should engrave this on our walls - permanently like a tattoo. This is why we should be thankful when we are entering into a store and someone whom we have no rapport kindly opens up the door. And it is just because they are judicious we can think we are auspicious but it has nothing to do with our luck or them being suspicious. There are tons of grateful persons who want to pass along a gesture and brighten someone's day, isn't that how we make the world better?

Lesson 13

Actions Must Match Intentions

We cannot say one thing
And then act contradictory
That's like running a failing business
And telling people it is a victory

Our intentions derive internally
Our actions are played out externally
If we really want true harmony
Then for harmony to last eternally

Our actions and our intentions
Need to most certainly match up
This will take some time to perfect
But it'll be worth so we don't erupt

Because the more we harmonize
The less time spent being inconsistent
If our actions don't match our intentions
We should consider ourselves nonexistent

Our actions and our intentions should always coexist congruently. We have all encountered a situation where our intentions were misconstrued and our actions were taken out of context – it can be upsetting, especially when the misinterpretation derives from someone dear to our hearts. If we say one thing and then do another we can be rightfully deemed fickle. This is due to the fact that we judge ourselves by our intentions while others judge us by our actions. If others are unaware of our intentions, they will naturally fill in the gaps between how we are presenting ourselves and what they believe our intentions to be. When our actions match our intentions we will feel a level of harmony that is unparalleled.

The harmonious sensation will derive from knowing that we are outwardly presenting ourselves in such an unadulterated manner that other folks can merely ascertain that everything we are saying and doing is the way in which we are intending to 'say' and 'do'. Because we are the most familiar with our intentions we may not place much value on how our actions are being perceived; but we should not assume that everyone is as aware of our intent as we are. We are in control of making sure that our actions and intentions are parallel, without placing all of our emphasis on how each of our words or actions are acknowledged. Although we should be open and truthful about what our intentions are, realistically, we have zero control over how we are perceived through the eyes of others; therefore, we should focus directly on everything within our span of control. Once our actions and intentions are aligned we should feel relieved that we are being honest with the world. We can then be self-assured that anything that comes out of our mouths is what we intended; every good deed that we display was intended; every promise that we make is intended; and so on and so forth.

We should note that when we are inconsistent in this aspect, no one would justly be able to trust or put his or her faith in us. Inversely, if someone continuously tells us one thing and does the complete opposite, would we place our trust or faith in them? Or would we have our reservations about their character and/or intentions? Remaining conscious of our intentions and how we present ourselves, and how we feel when others are inharmonious should help us to align our intentions and actions.

Lesson 14

What You Put Out, Comes Back

If we are our thoughts
And if we are our actions
What is put out and comes back
Becomes one like a contraction

What goes around comes around
Like a returning boomerang
The energy we put out comes back
Like retaliation from a gang

We reap what we sow
Is the biblical way to say it
Karma, Karma, Karma
Is how Buddhism claims it

But no matter our beliefs
It should be a relief
That we are in control
As if we are the chief

Just as our virtuousness will come back to us as recompense, as will our dishonesty and indecencies. Everything that we throw out into the world, so to speak, will come right back at us – the mysterious component is that we don't know when. This should give us further encouragement to act upright despite all of the negativity in the world. If we want to positivity to flow back to us, we need to then be outwardly positive. If we want kind deeds to flow back to us, we need to then perform kind deeds for others. If we want support and love to flow back to us, we need to outwardly show support and love. If we want happiness to flow back to us, we would need to outwardly showcase happiness. If we want honesty to flow back to us, we would then need to outwardly remain honest. If we want success to flow back to us, we would need to outwardly demonstrate our hard work, ambition, determination, and motivation. If we want solid friendships to flow back to us, we need to act as solid friends. If we genuinely want *anything* to flow back to us, then we need to genuinely portray it outwardly; if we are not genuine then what comes back around to us will not be genuine either.

If we smile at the world, the world will smile back and if we are truthful with the world; the world will be truthful back. If we frown at the world, the world will frown back and if we are deceitful to the world; the world will be deceitful back. If we ever begin to feel an undesirable energy following us around, we should analyze ourselves before we point fingers and distribute blame. What we find will be telling, as there will be congruence between our attitudes and what energy is being given back to us. And if we begin to feel a desirable energy following us around, we should still analyze ourselves to determine what is causing our affirmative outlook so that we can continue on and encourage others to have the same optimistic perspective.

The interesting element is that we are in full control over what comes back to us. This can be exciting and frightening depending on our mentalities and our level of comfort when it comes to taking full accountability for our lives. All in all, the energy that surrounds us is revealing of the energy that we present ourselves with.

Section III: Looking Forward

Lesson 1

El-Oh-Vee-E

We should enjoy life's bumpy roads
As we venture on our journey ahead
If we are ever feeling torn
We can pick up a needle and thread

And sew ourselves back together
Because there are storms we have to weather
Whether we like it or not
Our journey will not be as smooth as leather

But if love is at the forefront
We can confront every stop sign
And stop before every dead end
Turn around and continue our incline

Then we will feel inclined
To march forward with conviction
To leave behind the friction
And oversee and protect what's in our
jurisdiction

Looking forward is all about empowerment – taking accountability for and empowering our futures. Before we look forward though, we have to first acknowledge that our road ahead will not be silky smooth. Then, once we decide that *love* will lead us as we venture forward, we will be able to accept and learn from every situation that we are placed or thrown into. If we decide to be resentful of the people or barriers that we stumble upon on our journey, we will only create a disservice for ourselves. Embracing obstacles will ultimately allow for more personal growth and more personal growth allows for more wisdom.

Looking forward is about having a dream, setting some goals, living passionately and not selling our souls. It's about not having any excuses, not pointing fingers to blame, listening to our hearts and painting a picture to frame. The picture we are painting is the life we are portraying, the life we are creating, the life we are crocheting. With our hooked needle in hand, looking to create a pattern, which we hope will have a ring to it like the one around Saturn. It's about knowing our worth and coloring outside of the lines, until our picture is complete – one crayon at a time. It's about deleting our enemies and replacing them with allies and deleting anything that will possibly contribute to our demise. It's about having childlike fun and a wacky sense of humor, minding our own business and staying away from rumors. It's about having a plan and designing a roadmap, so that we can tackle the roadblocks and any other traps. It's about putting on a seatbelt and enjoying the ride, loving passionately and getting rid of our pride. Well, pride is not bad as long as no arrogance exists, we will lose all of our allies if arrogance persists. We do not need binoculars to see what lies ahead because if we follow our intuition we will not be misled. We have one life to live, one life to make, one life to die, one life to break. One story to create, we will write the foreword and the rest of chapters will follow on our journey forward.

Lesson 2

Have a Plan, Know Where You're Going

One direction, two directions
Three directions, four
Five directions, six directions
No directions more

Well, we clearly need a direction
But it has to be defined
And once we're headed on the right path
Our direction will become refined

If we do not know where we're going
We will follow someone else's path
How much fun do we think that'll be?
How long do we think it'll last?

Absent of having a plan for our futures, we would not have a clear direction on how to live our lives. Devising a plan will add both structure and purpose to our journey, and will always give us something to look forward to. This is not to say that spontaneity should not arise or be welcomed into our plan, but having an overall direction is essential. When we fail to design our own plan, we will naturally fall into a plan that someone else has created for us or into someone else's plan that they have created for themselves – neither option is desirable as they take away our control.

Remaining flexible while looking ahead is vital as we will need to confront and deal with the unexpected twists and turns on our journeys; and our journeys will most certainly have its twists and turns. The unpredictability of what will happen as we venture forward makes it even more necessary for us to have a plan. When we do not have a general direction to head towards, we can easily become overwhelmed and ultimately conquered by the emotions of dealing with unexpected events. Even when we do have a detailed plan the same can happen but if we continue to push forward so that we arrive at our goal(s), it will be easier to see past temporary circumstances that are deterring us from our general direction.

Within our plan, we are the narrator and main character of the story – this should always be the illustration! If we allow another person to star in our plan as the narrator or main character, it will no longer be *our* plan. We need to make sure that we are not consciously or subconsciously relinquishing control to someone who will then determine which direction we will take. All too often, we can become sucked into what other people think we should be doing, or taking a path that other people think we should take, or going in a general direction that other people think we should be going in. At the end of the day, it is wonderful to obtain feedback about our lives and where we are headed but we have to remain in control and create a path that works best for where it is we want to go.

Lesson 3

No Excuses

"My dog ate my homework"
"I can't", "I couldn't"
"I didn't know how to do it"
"I won't", "I shouldn't"

Woulda, shoulda, coulda
Excuses, excuses, excuses
Please save them for someone who cares
And enjoy being a nuisance

Excuses will not save the world
Excuses will not solve a crime
Excuses will not answer a problem
Excuses will not make us a dime

Please think of a time where making excuses has helped you to reach a goal? Please think of a time where someone else was making excuses and you enjoyed listening to them complain? Please think of a time where making excuses helped you to...you get the point! Making excuses are not beneficial on any level; to anyone; at any time; on any day! Excuses actually deter us away from taking accountability for our lives – there will always be someone or something to blame, but what good is allocating blame? We have come too far along in our lives to make excuses. As a matter of fact, excuses hold us back and if we are not careful, they can leave us behind and feeling stuck. This is due to the fact that making excuses is the easy way out. When we take full accountability for our lives and holistically embrace every situation that is happening to us, it requires added awareness – excuses do not require consciousness.

We can decide to make a habit out of making excuses or taking accountability, it is completely our choice. When we get in the habit of making excuses, we should take notice that none of our problems will be solved. When we get in the habit of taking accountability, we should take notice that our ability to be forthright and proactive will solve a considerable amount of our problems. Let's imagine a situation where we are in need of assistance, say with our cell phone provider for example. We call up the 1-800 number in order to figure out why our cell phone reception has been spotty and why our phone keeps shutting off in the middle of our conversations. After we explain our problem to the extremely courteous Customer Service Representative (CSR), he or she tells us that our reception is probably spotty because we are not using our phone near any of their towers. We are also told that our phone keeps turning off because we are probably hitting the 'power-off' button with our ear. We then reply that we always use our phone near their towers and there is no possible way that our ear could hit the 'power-off' button as it has to be held down for three seconds, and is also located on top of our phone; a place where our ear does not touch while we are on a call. The CSR then continues for another five to seven minutes rambling on with excuses about why our cell phone is not acting properly – now we are fuming; our patience has worn thin and our problem has not been solved. How thrilled would we have been if the CSR apologized for our inconveniences and either decided to troubleshoot our problem and/or place an order for a new or replacement phone? Had the latter occurred, we would have been spared aggravation and the CSR would have been spared minutes of yapping about excuses that we never wanted to listen to in the first place. So, will we decide to make excuses or take accountability?

Lesson 4

Know Your Worth

If you were a stock,
How much would you rise?
Would you contribute to a market crash?
Or take the market by surprise?

How much are you worth?
Could you tag it with a price?
Or is there no amount of money
That would be precise and suffice?

We are worth more than dollars
Our worth cannot be measured
By materialistic objects
Our worth should be treasured

Our worth is our value
Our value is our reassurance
Our reassurance is our faith
Our faith is our insurance

How do you feel when entering into an event filled with people? Confident? Insecure? Even-keeled? Overwhelmed? Poised? Withdrawn? Cautious? Intimidated? Absent of identifying ourselves as an extrovert or introvert, how significant and meaningful we feel speaks directly to our self-worth. How we feel about ourselves should not fluctuate depending on who we are around. A crowded room should not make us think any less of ourselves.

It is extremely important that we recognize our worth, not including our net worth or our assets although those are important as well – our worth meaning our value. Our level of self-worth will convey to the world how we view ourselves, which will in turn let the world know how it should view and treat us. Simply put, if we show (and believe) that we have an enormous amount of self-worth and that we have morals and standards, others will take notice and treat us accordingly. In the event that someone disregards our value and attempts to treat us with disrespect, we should show zero tolerance.

When we suffer from having low self-worth and self-esteem, unfortunately, it is outwardly detectible. Folks can sense when we are confident and sure of ourselves, and also when we are the opposite. There are individuals who intentionally prey on those with low-esteem as they are insecure and looking for someone to control – beware! The easiest approach to avoiding a run in with this type of manipulation is to remain consciously aware that we have value that cannot be stripped away from us. Thus, our value cannot be defined by possessions and money as both can be stripped away from us at any given time.

Once we begin to understand and show appreciation for our worth, we will increase our value and the respect that we receive from others. Most importantly, as our self-worth increases we will begin to feel rejuvenated and more excited about life as it will become more and more apparent that the world cherishes our value; that we have something *valuable* to offer to the world. There is no positive gain from showing oblivion or blatant disregard for our self-worth and letting others do the same. We should continuously focus on increasing, instead of decreasing, our worth.

Lesson 5

Create Allies, Not Enemies

Everywhere that we go
We have a chance to create an ally
We can also create an enemy
So what does this imply?

Allies will show support
Enemies will show hate
Allies accumulate rapport
Enemies accumulate bait

Not everyone will like us
We already know that is a fact
But the fact is we still have a choice
To build pacts with whom we attract

Each of us needs more allies
We will feel really warm with them
Having enemies will make us cold
So we should cough them up like phlegm

If we think of allies and enemies in terms of war, the more allies that we have the more resources and dominance we have available to ward off our enemies. If our amount of enemies outweighs our amount of allies, we should be concerned. The same applies in life, absent of war – we will never be in the best possible position if we have more enemies than allies. The old saying hints that we should 'keep our friends close but our enemies closer', but if we have an overabundance of enemies we will feel suffocated to say the least. It is our responsibility to genuinely create as many allies that we possibly can, as these individuals will support, encourage, push, rally around, and look out for us. In the same breath, we should make sure that we are acting as allies, for our allies, in order to show our loyalty. Having enemies is seemingly unavoidable but we do not have to openly welcome more into our lives.

The more allies that we have, the more confident we will feel, enemies will leave us feeling weak, and allies makes us as strong as steel. The more enemies that we have, the more paranoid we will become, allies keep up feeling whole, enemies spit us out like gum. On a grand scale, our allies can effortlessly work towards turning our enemies into allies. How it works is that those who support and believe in us can influence those who hate and cannot stand us. But why would we care if our enemies turn into allies? It's simple! We already know that there is no benefit of having enemies – sure, they can fuel us to be better and work harder with their constant hatred but our allies can also fuel us to be better and work harder with their constant support. Which is more soothing to pull from, hatred or support? The people who are against us do not deserve our energy or attention because it is discourteous to the people who are 100% for us. There is no harm in building more genuine relationships and bonds, as long as both sides are genuine; it will also pose as an opportunity to enhance our network.

Lesson 6

Appreciate The Rain, Literally and Figuratively

Drip, drop, drip, drop
Pitter-patter, pitter-patter
It's raining again, it's raining again
Spitter-splatter, spitter-splatter

The sun will come out tomorrow
Or maybe the day after
Might as well play in the rain
And turn our sorrows into laughter

Because we cannot stop the rain
An umbrella will help us temporarily
But why should we ward it off?
When a rainbow will show up momentarily

The rainbows are more than colors
Rainbows symbolize our hope
Bright colors come after darkness
That metaphor should help us cope

"Rain, rain, go away; come again another day! If you don't we cannot play!" But why can't we play in the rain? Is it harmful? If we learn to appreciate the rain, literally and figuratively, our lives will have more sunshine - pun intended. Literally speaking, rain is inevitable; trees, plants, and harvests all need water in order to grow and stay healthy; we need oxygen and food in order to grow and stay healthy as well. Figuratively speaking, rain is inevitable; trials, tribulations, and obstacles all need to occur in order for us to learn and grow. So why is it that we hate the rain so much? Rain is beautiful depending on the angle at which we are looking at it. If we can view rain as a necessity that benefits nature and our well-being, we can learn to love the rain; the serenity that it brings, the song that it sings, while it runs down our window pane and then flies without wings.

After or during each rainstorm a rainbow always appears and we can use this as a sign that the sun will come out again. As necessary as rain is for survival, it doesn't last. Figuratively speaking, the storms won't last – we have to do our part in weathering the storms and looking past the rain. Without knowing when the rain will stop, simply knowing that it will one day stop should encourage us to keep pushing forward. Sometimes it may feel like we experience constant torrential downpours; this should not stop us from dancing in the rain. With our rain boots on our feet and our rain jackets on our backs, and the rain falling down we should enjoy and relax.

Literally speaking, rainy days seem to bring about slight depression in some people. These individuals feel overly sluggish when it rains and complain nonstop about how badly they do not want to step outside of the house; or about how they don't want their clothes or hair to get wet. It's true that rainy weather can be exhausting...if we allow it to be! Dark clouds may accompany the rain but the color of the clouds does not need to reflect our moods. Should we only be happy when it is sunny and sad when it is raining? Life does not stop because of rain; life begins after the last drop falls!

Lesson 7

You Can Learn From Anyone

Age is certainly just a number
Wisdom is also held by the youth
Little children are the purest creations
Hence, they are closer to the truth

We should not dismiss a lesson
Because we do not like the teacher
We can learn from everyone
From a criminal to a preacher

From a child to the elderly
From the corner to a college
From a friend to a stranger
Anyone can kick a little knowledge

We just have to pay attention
And open ourselves up to receive
Without us being judgmental
And holding stereotypes up our sleeve

If we open ourselves up to potentially acquiring knowledge from anyone, we will be completely astonished by everything that we would learn. We are all teachers in our own way, with or without a formal educational background to back us up. We each have a story to tell and each story has a multitude of lessons attached to it. This means that each of us, as the narrator, is responsible for sharing our story. The interesting aspect of operating as the narrator is that we may not even recognize that we are teaching. Regardless of if we recognize it though, we are always teaching a lesson to someone. In the same token, just as much as we are teachers we are also students. Being on both sides of the spectrum will be advantageous and assist us with our overall growth.

It is effortless for us to stick with learning from those in which we are already familiar; but we won't grow this way. It can be easy to judge someone based off of the way that he or she speaks or dresses and gather that there is absolutely no way that we can learn anything from them; but we won't grow this way. It can be easy to discount what someone is saying based off of his or her age; but we won't grow this way. It can be easy to ignore or not engage a person in conversation that has a different background than we do; but we will not grow this way. It can be easy to look down upon a person who lives in a neighborhood that we consider undesirable; but we will not grow this way. Regardless of our age, religious or political affiliations, occupations, place of residence, hobbies, or interests in music, we can all learn from one another.

The key to learning from anyone is to get rid of our judgmental and stereotypical attitudes. Every time that we interact with someone, we are either teaching or being taught, sometimes both. Even when we are not interacting, we can still learn if we are open to it. The person who is driving the speed limit in the car in front of us while we are in an extreme rush is teaching us to be more patient. The child in the room who is laughing and giggling while we are in a somber mood is teaching us to perk up because we have far more reasons to smile than to frown. The abusive relationship that we have seen a friend/relative involved in or the one that we have been in ourselves has taught us inner strength. The micromanaging and insecure boss has taught us strength and tolerance, and how we should not allow anyone to project their controlling and insecure ways upon us. The absentee parent has taught us forgiveness. The person who cheated on us taught us how to overcome heartache and still feel comfortable with vulnerability. The job that we interviewed and were not hired for taught us that everything that is meant to happen will happen. The time that we locked our keys in our car
taught us to slow down and pay attention. The last funeral that we attended taught us that we

should cherish life's every moment because it will one day come to an end.

Lesson 8

Give Your All or Nothing

If we will only give 50 percent
While someone else will give 110
Then that will be the difference
Between who will lose and who will win

Giving 110 isn't a guarantee
That we will always be number one
But it does increase our odds
To something from none

But why should we start a project?
Or sign ourselves up to play a sport?
If we will not give it our all?
We will always come up short

There will always be a person
Who would love to take our place
So we should not make it easy
For us to be replaced

When we are investing our time in a venture or relationship of any type, we will see greater results or have a more rewarding relationship by always giving our all. If we give a small percentage of our time/energy and still expect to be rewarded as if we gave 100 percent, we will be sadly mistaken and disappointed. With this, we should also recognize when giving our all is not being appreciated or is not leading us in a desirable direction. We can never be steered wrong by giving our best but if we are not being met half way in a relationship or receiving the results that we would like from a venture, we should accept that we tried our best and move on.

Giving our all does not guarantee that we will be the best or that we will be the most successful but it does not have to. Our dedication and enthusiasm solidifies that we will never ever give up; no one can take that away from us. When we give half effort, dedication, and enthusiasm we will receive subpar results in return. But if we give half effort we need to ask ourselves why we are giving any effort at all; giving half effort is essentially identical to giving no effort. When we want to accomplish a great feat we have to work so hard that our ambition may scare us, but in a good way. When we want to have the most rewarding relationships we have to love so deeply that our affection may scare us, but in a good way.

When we genuinely focus on giving life

all that we have and not the rewards that come along with our efforts, we will have already been rewarded. Of course it is natural to think about recompense and our goals coming to culmination. We should not put all of our energy into something or someone without receiving or expecting energy back but it should not be our main focus. When we focus more on the benefits rather than the effort that we are putting forth, we will always be dissatisfied.

Lesson 9

Dream Big or Don't Dream At All

We should all have a dream
It will give us a reason to fight
But not with two fists in the air
We will fight with all our might

To have our dream come to fruition
This is our important mission
If we multiply our ambition
We will have enough ammunition

To make the impossible come true
Our dreams should frighten us a little
From being larger than we can imagine
Over the rainbow and past the skittles

If our dreams are really small
We should not even dream at all
They say we should crawl before we walk
But we should dream before we crawl

Just as we should give our all or give nothing at all, we should also dream big or don't dream at all. Having a dream allows us to create synergy with our imagination and reality. Making our dreams come true gives us a chance to not only astonish the world but to astonish ourselves as well. We have one life to make all of our dreams come true so we do not have time to waste. Since we only have a limited amount of time to have our dreams come to fruition, our dreams should be big – so big that we do not know where to begin with making them come true – so big that we receive shocked expressions when we share our dreams with others – so big that it takes years of constant motivation and concentration to start picking up true momentum – so big that when our dreams finally come true we feel like we are on top of the world!

To live without dreaming is like being a con artist without scheming or having a coupon without redeeming or having a kettle without steaming. Dreaming is a necessity because it keeps us wide-awake like an earthquake that shakes and shakes and shakes. Our dreams may seem impossible at first and even complex but we have to fight until our death like Malcolm X. We can dream while we are asleep, wake up and make them come true like we stumbled upon a discovery but it's our own breakthrough. Our dreams should be vivid, colorful, and bright so they shine and beam like a light that is white. Not 'lite bright' the game, light bright like the sun that is so luminous and iridescent the glow cannot come undone. We need the light to direct us while our dreams perfect us, and we encourage other dreamers and our dreams connect us.

Dreaming big also allows us to test out and stretch our limits. How far are we willing to go? Will we give up on our dreams? Will we give up on ourselves? Will we be overcome by fear? Will we be discouraged by failure? Will we be afraid of success? How much are we willing to sacrifice? Do we believe in our dreams enough? Do others believe in our dreams? Are we giving our all? How bad do we want it? How bad do you want it?

Lesson 10

Listen To Your Heart

Our hearts will tell our story
If we can buckle down and listen
It will tell us how to stay together
So we don't separate like division

To not separate from our inner voice
To not separate from our intention
To not separate from how it feels
To not separate from our intuition

Our hearts will play our song
Will we choose to sing along?
Or will we drown out all the noise
Or hear it as loudly as a gong?

We each have a little voice inside of us that speaks to us constantly; we can call it inner voice, intuition, or instincts but ultimately it is our heart that is speaking. Although not located in the center, our heart is the core of our being. It aches, it breaks but it makes no mistakes as it heals, it feels, and allows us to fall head over heels. Our hearts pump oxygen throughout our body and pump our story into the atmosphere, so as long as we follow our hearts with our every decision. We will know what our heart is saying by the sensations that we feel and the smiles we can't conceal when everything is going smoothly like the skin on an eel. Our hearts will lead us towards the path that we are meant to follow, and will guide us the entire time if we give our consent. Our hearts will never lead us down a dark and stormy road for us to stand there, stuck, watching all the drama unfold. We will be guided, carefully, thoughtfully, and with the tools for careful, thoughtful, guidance to make it through.

The only times that our hearts will not lead the way is when we decide to stop listening; when we begin to second guess ourselves and go against our better judgment. Although we can learn valuable lessons from not following our hearts, we can also avoid the repercussions by not going astray from what we know and feel is right. We have already acknowledged that in order to live a worthwhile life, love has to be at the forefront and there is nothing that symbolizes love more than our hearts. Following our hearts forces us to rely heavily on faith; not only faith in a higher power but also faith in ourselves. It means believing that our hearts are always telling us the truth and discarding any lies, while teaching us a lesson every time that our heart cries. The pain is not for nothing; the pain is for a reason because it strengthens up our heart and prepares us for any season.

When we make the decision to listen to our heart there is not one external force that can drown out the sound. We should not allow anyone or anything to interfere with what our hearts are telling us. We move away from our authenticity each time that we allow an external interference. Although we have close bonds with the individuals within our inner circle, none of them can lead us in a better direction than our hearts can. We have to rely on our hearts from the start to the finish so our loyalty to ourselves and our truth do not diminish.

Lesson 11

Have a Sense of Humor

Laughter is the best medicine
It will cure us of our pain
We can take one laughing pill a day
And it will dissolve and keep us sane

We can frown as if we are sad
We can yell as if we are mad
We can laugh as if we are glad
And be led by laughter like a fad

Laughing until our stomach hurts
Laughing until there are tears shed
Laughing until we cannot breathe
Laughing until our laughter spreads

Having a sense of humor will help to wash our pain away, as it acknowledges that we will soon be confronted with brighter days. Being able to laugh at ourselves is a sign of maturity because it shows that we are secure and have rid ourselves of insecurity. Alone, a sense of humor can make a situation light-hearted because it lightens up the mood and gets any party started. Who wants company that is uptight? Who aren't flexible but rather upright? And who thinks that having fun is wrong when it's all right, alright?

We will find that if we take life too seriously, we are simultaneously limiting our ability to have fun and enjoy what is happening around us. Absent of having a sense of humor, we will also find that we are constantly tense, stressed out, and/or unhappy. A sense a humor should not give the impression that we interpret everything in jest or that there is absolutely no situation or person that should be taken seriously but it does show that we are capable of seeing life from a different angle. Life will throw us many curveballs, how we deal with them is indicative of our perspective. Will we cry because we struck out? Will we become angry if we swing and miss? Or will we giggle at how we swung and missed and concentrate on how to hit a homerun on the next pitch? Giggling does not deem us insensitive, frivolous, or unfocused but displays that we are our enjoying our ride.

We do not have to be a comedian to have a sense of humor – it is not about telling jokes or always being in the limelight or life of the party. We don't even have to be around other people to display our sense of humor. A great sense of humor will ultimately better our health; this is not to say that a sense of humor will cure diseases, infections, or terminal illnesses but it will absolutely assist us with our feelings of restoration. Smiling or pouting? Calmness or shouting? Laughing or bawling? Our sense of humor is calling! Of course, sadness and crying are a part of life too but will humor or misery help us to pull through?

Lesson 12

The Power of Positivity

Don't underestimate the power of positivity
A great attitude will serve you well
Your bright smile will help others
Even if you can't tell

Positive versus negative
Optimistic versus pessimistic
Which side will win the battle?
Your choice should be simplistic

A positive attitude opens doors
A negative attitude slams it shut
A negative attitude holds you back
A positive attitude frees you up

A positive attitude can be learned
A negative attitude can be learned
A positive attitude can build a bridge
A negative attitude leaves it burned

Upholding a positive attitude is a choice that each of us can make. Upholding a negative attitude is also a choice that each of us can make. If we weigh the benefits of having a positive or negative attitude we will find that while both are powerful, positivity is far more effective for our happiness and for making the world a better place. When negativity enters into our space, it harmfully clouds the air that we are breathing in. Not literally so to speak but it does pollute the world as it is unconstructive and draining. Positivity on the other hand contributes to the air quality; when we breathe it into our lungs it is refreshing and causes a contagious chain reaction of positive behaviors. A chain reaction of positivity can wrap itself around the world, multiple times, and touch so many lives once it arrives. How many lives has negativity changed for the better? What if we wore negativity as if it was a trendsetter? We would be so miserable, cranky, and depressed; and all of the positive people would hate the way we were dressed. But we each have to express and confess in the mirror whether positivity or negativity will make our vision clearer.

Positive people tend to attract positive people and positive energy, and negative people tend to attract negative people and negative energy; what type of people and energy would you like to attract? Misery loves company but so does elation; misery is the cause of depression, elation is the cause of celebration. If it is a party, we all can be sent an invite as long as we have foresight that positivity should be forthright. Whether we decide to have a positive or negative attitude, it will be noticeable to the world because a positive attitude is uplifting and a negative attitude is draining; a positive attitude brings out solutions and a negative attitude brings out complaining. Both a positive and negative attitude will attract more friends but a positive attitude will build our ties while a negative attitude will make ties end. A positive attitude will get us ahead, a negative attitude will leave us behind; a positive attitude will open our eyes and a negative attitude will leave us blind. Because we will be unable to see all of the positivity going around if we are too busy sulking and being drowned by our frown.

Lesson 13

You Cannot Do It Alone

We all wish it was that easy
But success is something else
We can aim for the stars
But can't do it by ourselves

We need someone to push us
We may not like to be pushed but
Without a little push and shove
When push comes to shove, then what?

No matter where we want to go in life, we need a solid support system to continuously encourage and keep us on the right track. Hence why it is vital that we have more allies than enemies and that we do not drain our inner circle, as well as the inverse. We can ask any person who we deem successful about his or her journey to success and if they are humble, they will tell us about the people who aided them along the way, amongst other specifics. Every coach needs a coach, every mentor needs a mentor, every therapist needs a therapist, every doctor needs a doctor, every teacher needs a teacher; the point is that we all need guidance. On the opposite side of the spectrum, we still cannot do it alone; we need to share our success and journeys with others. We can go ahead and impact the world, which would be magnificent. In getting and gaining we become successful, but only in helping others will we become significant.

If we think back to any of our accomplishments, there was at least one person who cheered us on and encouraged us to never give up. Absent of helpful resources and a support system, success is nearly impossible. Absent of success, and on a day-to-day basis, we still need a support system. Knowing this, we should not be too ashamed to ask for assistance when we need it; whether we need help with parenting, reaching a goal, goal setting, learning a new skill, finding a job – the list can continue on indefinitely. We are all in this world to help one another so we should not be offended or discouraged that we cannot do it alone. We all need a shoulder to cry on, a shoulder to lean on, a shoulder to stand on, and a shoulder to tap on. The quicker that we embrace this notion, the better off our lives and the world will be.

Lesson 14

Pay It Forward

You are who you are
Because of the people who came before you
You are who you are
Because of their point of view

Because of their will to fight
Because of their will to battle
Because of their determination
They couldn't be shaken like a rattle

Because life was their teacher
Because they were the only students
Who actually listened and learned
And who remained prudent

For it is they who made it easier
We should pay homage to our roots
For their drive and their service
We can now labor for our fruits

The best way that we can pay homage to our roots is by 'paying it forward' – to pass along the knowledge, or empathy, or gratitude, or gesture, or compliment, or favor, or wisdom, or any other mechanisms that have assisted us in becoming who we are today. By paying it forward, we are not only thanking the individuals who have helped us but also aiding someone else along their journey. Paying it forward also shows our true appreciation and thankfulness for the world, for our struggles, and for the ability to help someone just as we were helped.

Paying it forward should be bestowed genuinely as it has nothing to do with receiving good fortune in return. Alone, it should help us to feel great about ourselves as we are personally contributing to making the world a better place. Others will be appreciative that we are helping, and will then pay it forward to someone else, who will then pay it forward to someone else, who will then pay it forward to someone else.

Since we know that we cannot reach any level of success alone, there should be no reason why we cannot pay it forward – no reason whatsoever! Where would we be if no one took the time to explain things to us, step-by-step? Where would we be if someone didn't show us the ropes...the keys to life? Where would we be if someone didn't assist us with feeling welcomed in a new job, team, etc.? Where would we be if someone didn't help us during the most trying times in our life? Where would we be if no one showed patience with us? If no one believed in us? If no one assisted us during a financial crisis? Where would we be if someone didn't pay it forward to help us?

Lesson 15

We Are All Connected

Six degrees of separation
Is all it takes to connect the world
You know him, he knows her
The relationships are twirled

So and so and so and so
Used to date our bosses' brother
Then, so and so and so and so
Worked with our best friend's mother

We could originally be from the South
And run into someone in the West
On a family vacation or business trip
And they pass the six-degree test

Thus we can now conclude
All of our energies should be respected
So when we leave our lasting impression
Remember that we are all connected

We are sitting around with a group of friends and someone asks a peculiar question. We debate back and forth about what the answer might be until one of our tech savvy friends decides to settle it once and for all – via his or her smartphone! They go onto the Internet and find their favorite search engine; and as they begin to type the question in, four or five searchable options pop up – one being the unusual question that we were just debating about. Voilà, ten pages of results filled with the answer we were just looking for. But how can that be? Who else would think of that question? The answer is simple; we are all connected.

We will realize just how connected we all are each time that we are interacting with someone. Whether we share similar hobbies, similar careers paths, similar childhood upbringings, similar passions, similar tastes in music, similar tastes in food, similar stories of past heartaches, similar struggles, a similar purpose, or similar journeys onward. If we find that we are not directly connected via our interactions, we will surely find that we are connected by six degrees of separation or less. This is an indication that all of our energies are connected. That would then indicate why we should respect and cherish our every interaction, no matter how short, long, frequent, or scarce they may be. This also strengthens the case for having more allies than enemies, as we never know how our enemies will resurface, who is in their inner circle and how we are all ultimately connected.

It's a small world after all! Of all the billions of people in the world, we are all somehow connected. That can be exciting and chilling; it should also make us eager to rid ourselves of our judgmental ways and negativity as our energies are connected with and impact numerous people.

Lesson 16

Color Outside The Lines

Coloring inside of the lines
Sure makes for a pretty photo
That we can hang on our fridge
And it will sit there just like Toto

But in order to create a masterpiece
We need to color outside the lines
Sometimes we have to stretch the rules
Instead of staying in the confines

Pretty doesn't mean it's perfect
Perfect doesn't even exist
We should scribble all over the paper
Until the world feels our gist

Starting in our youth, we have been taught to literally color inside of the lines. For us not to make a mess by scribbling and to be sure that we used the outline of our picture as a guide for coloring. While this may have been useful in teaching us the dynamics of structure and neatness it is not so helpful in looking forward. Structure and being neat are necessary but coloring inside of the lines is not. Sometimes we have to stretch the boundaries and color all over our canvas in order to create our masterpiece – the boundaries being the norm, the canvas being our lives, the masterpiece being our legacy.

We are too unique to mimic someone else's masterpiece, we need to create our own; the world needs us to. After we tap into our creativity, purpose, and desire we can begin to color. The masterpiece that we are creating is our story. As long as we are living, we are still coloring and creating our work of art. Once we gain more wisdom and experience, our masterpiece will begin to come together. The beginning stages will look like a work in progress, which we are as well. The more that we learn about ourselves, other people, and life in general the more inspiration that we will gain for our picture. There is no telling what we can achieve with our inspiration.

As long as we understand that our masterpiece will not be perfect, we should feel no pressure. If we spend our lives trying to create a perfect picture, we will be continuously disappointed. If we spend our lives trying to create a picture that other people will enjoy, we will be continuously disappointed. If we spend our lives trying to create a picture that does not truthfully depict our story, we will be continuously disappointed. If we spend our lives trying to create a picture that someone else has already outlined for us, we will be continuously disappointed. Our picture has to be colored with authenticity, with passion, and outside of the lines.

Lesson 17

Live With Passion

What is love without passion?
What is success without passion?
What is life without passion?
What is passion without passion?

Passion is our burning desire
Passion is our intense emotions
Passion will confidently keep us going
If our passion is as wide as an ocean

If our passion roars like a lion
If our passion sparkles like the stars
If our passion is mystical like a forest
If our passion has 'drive' like a car

What is love without passion?
What is success without passion?
What is life without passion?
What is passion without passion?

Love without passion is not love. Success without passion is not success. Life without passion is not life. Passion without passion is not passion. If we are not living and loving passionately we should reevaluate our approach. Passion gets us started, keeps us going, and inspires others to be passionate. Passion is the burning desire inside of us – we each have it, we just have to tap into it. We can identify passion by the way it makes us feel; how it effortlessly energizes us and keeps us smiling. When we dream big and color outside of the lines, while maintaining passion, a positive attitude, and a sense of humor we could astound the world. The areas in which we are passionate will always be the areas where our passion lies, as passion does not die. We may experience passionate intimate love with multiple people throughout the course of our lives, for example, and although the passion did not remain with the same person, our passion still remained in the area of intimate love. The same applies for when we have a particular strength that we have identified, when combined with passion we are adding depth to our masterpiece. We may experience different levels of passion depending on what we are doing and how open we are to receiving all of the passion that we have to offer the world.

Not only does passion energize us and keep us smiling, but it also keeps us feeling confident and invigorated while it keeps our minds sharp. When we are passionate, truly passionate, we are constantly thinking of new ideas to increase and expand our desire. No one can take away our passion and because it is such a strong emotion, even if our paths lead us away from our passion temporarily, it will always await us when we are ready to return to it. Our passion will easily separate us from those who give minimal effort with zero desire. Our passion will also separate us from those who are not in tune with their emotions. Because passion is so beneficial and influential it will drive us into territories that are both familiar and unfamiliar; as long as we switch gears to park every once in a while and take in what is going on all around us, we will feel refreshed and appreciative.

Lesson 18

Ask and You Shall Receive (But Be Open To Receiving)

"I want this, I want that"
"Can I have it? Can I have it?"
"I need this, I need that"
"Can I grab it? Can I grab it?"

We always, always want
But are we always, always open
To receiving what it is we want
Or have we forgotten the notion?

That if we ask, it will come
But we should be careful for what we ask
Because it can take us by surprise
Similar to someone in a scary mask

But it should not cause horror
Since we spoke it into existence
Before we ask for another thing
We need to be open and not show resistance

We can speak what we want into existence if we ask for it, sounds simple enough – we want it, we ask for it, we receive it. How could we complicate this? The answer is simpler than the concept – 1) if we ask and are not ready to receive and 2) when we ask and become impatient because we did not receive what we wanted, when we wanted. Part of being faithful is understanding that every piece in our life's puzzle will fall into place at the right moment, with the right people surrounding us, with the right tools to prepare us, right when we need it. Needing versus wanting can be obscure if we are not vigilant in defining what the differences are. Needing signifies necessity, meaning it is a *requirement* to enhance our lives. Wanting signifies craving, meaning it would be *enjoyable* to have but it is not necessary to enhance our lives.

We are aware that we should be careful about what we ask for but we should be even more aware that we ought to be open to what we are looking to receive. Many times we ask for the same thing so often that when it finally comes to us we have not prepared ourselves to receive it – but why? The preparation of receiving is far more involved than the seamless task of asking. But if we have not opened ourselves up to receive, what is the point in asking? Before we open our mouths to ask, we need to first prepare ourselves to receive so that no surprises will follow. We will essentially work backwards – open ourselves up to receive and then ask for what it is we want to receive. In the reverse process, we can take as long as we need to organize our thoughts and thoroughly prepare ourselves.

In the same breath, we have to also understand that we cannot become impatient if we are not receiving on the timeline in which we have created. Things will happen when they are supposed to! So while it is wise to still prepare before asking, we must be alert to the fact that we do not know when our time to receive will be. This is essentially congruent with the belief that although tomorrow isn't promised we should still plan for the future. Knowing this, we can always do our part in planning ahead and opening up to what the world has in store for us.

Lesson 19

Reflection + Introspection

Now you have reached the end
Of this book but not your journey
You have read some of the laws of life
And you do not have to be an attorney

To study and pass the bar
The bar that life has set
You can listen and play it back
As if life is a cassette

But even a cassette has to end
It can only hold so much content
Our lives will also end one day
Without us giving our consent

But while we are still here
In order to not feel any disconnection
We will continuously need to practice
Reflection and introspection

Our journey does not end here, we have more mileage to gain, more wisdom to consume, more reasons to sip on champagne[2]. And toast to our losses and drink to our successes because we got rid of the negativity as well as our stresses. Reflecting on the past will help us look into our future, and stare it right in the eyes as our wounds have been sutured. We are not scared, we are not afraid; we can walk ahead as if we are in a promenade. We should continue to introspect, and stare straight into the mirror until our vision becomes clearer and our truth appears nearer. We do not know it all and actually we never will, yet we should absorb as much as we can and continue our journey uphill. The inner war is now over but the battle is just starting, our new persona is building and our old one departing. Of course we are the same person but our spirit now revels because we have freed ourselves up and warded off the devils. Absent of religion, a devil meaning any evil that has entered into our soul looking for retrieval. But we gave it an eviction notice because we are in control, it cannot live here anymore there is no need to cajole. Looking internally should be a given and become habitual, no formal ceremonies necessary we don't need a ritual. What we need is to love, and to love, and to love, and when love is thrown our way we catch it in our glove. And place it inside of our hearts so it opens up and beats louder and louder and

---

[2] If we are of the legal drinking age!

louder until we are pleased and prouder. With who we are becoming, with the life we are leading because we are now a leader and have indefinitely stopped the bleeding. Our blood is still flowing but our blood is not leaking from the bottom of our hearts and our hearts are not seeking. Because we have given it what it needs to be whole and to be pure, we don't need anyone to reassure, as we know it for sure. We must keep marching on and keep adding to our story, which will add to our happiness and add to our glory. Since our story has begun and we already wrote the foreword, we can love inward, live outward, and look forward.

Become A Pro:
Please don't live with any regrets!
Let it go! Let it go!
Still living in the past?
Say it ain't so! Say it ain't so!
Your path is getting bumpy?
Let it flow! Let it flow!
Wish you knew better back then?
How would you know? How would you know?
You are one unique individual!
No Average Joe! No Average Joe!
Feel like you are suffocating?
Inhale and blow! Inhale and blow!
Feel like you are going fast?
Just go slow! Just go slow!
Feel like your grass is not green?
Water and mow! Water and mow!
Look down the hall into your future!
Beyond status quo! Status quo!
The present is still a gift!
Tie the bow! Tie the bow!
Try your best every day!
Rain, sleet, or snow! Rain, sleet, or snow!
Keep on making mistakes!
It's how you grow! How you grow!
If you get stuck in a ditch,
Call for a tow! Call for a tow!
You are THE main attraction!
Star of the show! Star of the show!
Do you want control over your life?
Yes or no? Yes or no?
Loving inward, living outward, looking forward!
Become a pro!

Be Vulnerable:
Oh I know, don't I know!
Being vulnerable is tough
But there is nothing beneficial
About being guarded and closed up

Think back to years and years ago
I'm talking many, many moons
When you were just a little toddler
Watching cartoons in the afternoon

Were you thinking of getting hurt?
C'mon, please tell me the truth!
You were thinking of drinking milk
And about getting your first tooth

So when did you become concerned
With vulnerability and being overt?
Hmm, maybe when life happened?
Maybe from the first time you were hurt?

Or maybe, oh maybe, maybe
When you realized it was "safer"
To walk through life being guarded
Ready to crack like a little wafer

You will need to learn vulnerability
If you want to experience love
I mean the kind that makes you weak
And lifts you above and above and above

Not just in your intimate relationships
But with co-workers, fam, and friends

You need to practice being open
Until you feel you have been cleansed

Of all the bad habits that you learned
Because there is power in vulnerability
Not just because of humility
But also because of tranquility

See, I'm learning to be vulnerable
If I get hurt, I will be fine
Because I have plenty of great girlfriends
And plenty of vintage wine

There are true benefits of being hurt
Think about all the important lessons
That you will walk away with
You'd be ready like a delicatessen

To open up and stay focused
So please pull down your defenses
You cannot learn and enjoy life
When there are walls around your senses
Please come to a consensus
And break down all of your fences
When your vulnerability dispenses
Is when your life actually commences
Now, do you get it?

I Am Free, I Am Me:

I can breathe. I can feel. I am free. I am me.
I can laugh. I can cry but I am free because I am me.
I can hurt but I can fly because I am free. I am me.
I can fall down but get back up because I am free. I am me.
I am not perfect. I am flawed but I am free because I am me.
I make mistakes - lots of them but I am free. I am me.
I am not a prisoner of who you want me to be because I am free. I am me.
I can jump and be afraid but I am free. I am me.
I can feel lonely but I am not alone. I am free. I am me.
I am unchained from my past. I am free. I am free.
I know a lot. I don't know it all but I am free. I am me.
I have scars and bumps and bruises but I am free because I am me.
I can now look ahead with clarity because I am free. I am me.
I can be open. I can be vulnerable because I am free. I am me.
I can move any hurdle or mountain because I am free. I am me.
Would you agree that you can see that I am free because I am me?
I do not care because I am here because I am free, I am me!

Nurture Your Inner Child:
Inside of all of us lives a child. This is the child who was never given the opportunity to fully develop and grow. This child is still scared of being hurt. This child is still worried that he or she is not good enough. This child still wants to be liked by everyone that he or she comes in contact with. This child is still scared of neglect and being alone. This child never received enough hugs. This child never received enough love. This child is sad. This child is angry. This child has anxiety. This child still feels the pain of empty promises. This child is awakened at night by agonizing flashbacks. This child was made fun of. This child was bullied. This child lived in disarray. This child was forced to take on adult responsibilities when he or she barely knew how to just be...a child. This child never received the praise that they thought they deserved. This child struggled to find its identity. This child was never heard. This child was never understood. This child still seeks attention and when this child is not properly nurtured, he or she acts out. This child still cries. The sounds of the cries are too loud and too painful for this grown up child to handle. So this grown child ignores the young child that lives insides of him or her. Both are uncomfortable, both are misunderstood, both cry out. But until this little child is nurtured the grown up will never grow up! Please love this child, listen to this child, soothe this child, talk to this child, tell this child that you understand them. Let this child know that you will never leave its side. This child needs you – nurture this child with all that you have and you both will grow; as one!